D0908767

DATE DUE

Twayne's English Authors Series

EDITOR OF THIS VOLUME

Kinley Roby

Northeastern University

Denis Johnston

TEAS 230

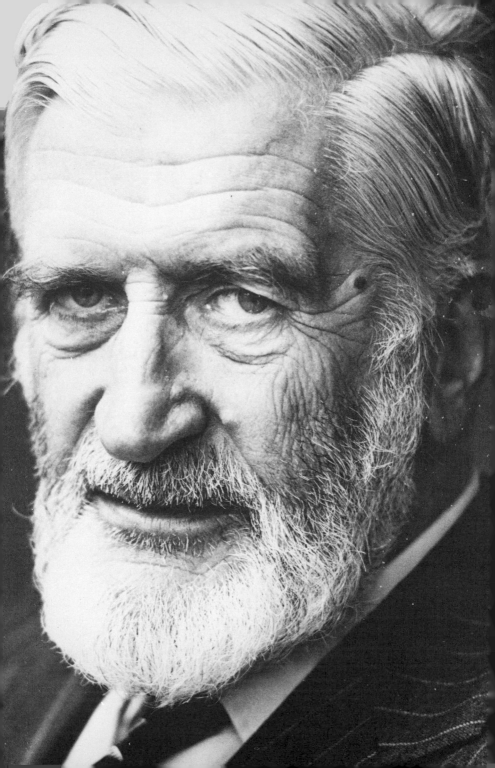

DENIS JOHNSTON

By GENE A. BARNETT

Fairleigh Dickinson University

TWAYNE PUBLISHERS
A DIVISION OF G. K. HALL & CO., BOSTON

Library of Congress Cataloging in Publication Data

Barnett, Gene Austin.
    Denis Johnston.

    (Twayne's English authors series ; TEAS 230)
    Bibliography: p. 163–66
    Includes index.
    1. Johnston, Denis, 1901–   —Criticism and
interpretation.
PR6019.0397Z6   822'.9'12   78–8018
ISBN 0–8057–6701–0

Frontispiece photo of Denis Johnston by Fergus Bourke,
courtesy of the Abbey Theatre.

For Marj

Contents

About the Author

Gene A. Barnett, a native of Missouri, is a graduate of three midwestern universities. He received the Bachelor of Arts from Oklahoma Baptist University and the Master of Arts from the University of Oklahoma. His doctorate is from the University of Wisconsin where he specialized in American Literature and wrote his dissertation on Hawthorne under the mentorship of the late Professor Harry Hayden Clark. He has published articles on Hawthorne, Robert Bolt, and George Bernard Shaw in such periodicals as *Studies in Romanticism, The Dalhousie Review* and the *Ball State University Forum.* He began his teaching carrer at Wayne State University in Detroit where he taught courses in modern drama and Shakespeare. In 1967, he accepted a teaching position at Fairleigh Dickinson University, Teaneck-Hackensack Campus, where he currently teaches courses in modern drama, the history of drama, Shakespeare, and comparative literature. He spent two years in the U.S. Army Security Agency, and during the last fifteen years he has traveled frequently in Europe and as far afield as Japan, Egypt, Iran, India and Nepal. Such trips have enabled him to keep abreast of developments in contemporary theatre, especially in England where he sometimes sees as many as eleven performances a week. He is also interested in classic theatre and has visited the sites of several Greek and Roman theatres in Italy, Sicily and Greece. He is an informed viewer of opera and is also interested in art and antiques. He lives in Teaneck, New Jersey.

Preface

In the summer of 1898, William Butler Yeats, Lady Augusta Gregory, and Edward Martyn jointly agreed on a repertory of two plays
for the Irish Literary Theatre which they would formally organize
the following January. Between May 8 and 13 of 1899, seven performances of Yeats' *The Countess Cathleen* and Martyn's *The
Heather Field* were given in repertory, and with these "small, half-
casual, half-heroic beginnings," the Irish Dramatic Movement was
initiated.[1] Between a second season in February of 1900 and the
third in October of the following year, Denis Johnston was born
(June 18, 1901). Twenty-five years later, he offered his first play,
Shadowdance, to the world-famous Abbey Theatre, an offspring
of the Irish Literary Theatre. After revisions and a new title, Yeats
and Lady Gregory, still directors of the Abbey Theatre, rejected the
play. Yet with this rejection, Johnston's career as a dramatist was
launched. The work that Lady Gregory found, for the most part,
"rather common," and that Yeats had advised the young barrister-
playwright to simplify and shorten, was revised counter to Yeats'
instructions and given to the new Gate Theatre for production with
yet another title. Almost four decades later, the manager-director
of the Abbey, Ernest Blythe, wrote that the "only case in which the
Abbey definitely failed to produce a play of high merit which had
been submitted to it, was that of Denis Johnston's satirical fantasy,
The Old Lady Says "No!"[2]

It is unfortunate that Denis Johnston's plays are not often produced, because his work for the theater constitutes a significant
achievement which, in the generation of Irish dramatists that came
to maturity in the 1920s and 1930s, can be matched only by Sean
O'Casey. The present study has three primary aims: to revive an
interest in Johnston's work by examining the relevance, range, and
quality of his *oeuvre;* to clarify his position within the historical
context of the Irish theater; and to demonstrate his ability to trans-
cend the limitations of a strictly nationalist drama. The plays, with
one exception, are discussed chronologically. *Nine Rivers from
Jordan,* a spiritual autobiography of the World War II years, is

given special consideration, for in several ways it is an important supplement to an examination of the plays. The importance for the present study of two critical works on John M. Synge and Jonathan Swift, as well as a privately published philosophical work, *The Brazen Horn,* is not such as to necessitate detailed discussion, although they are referred to at appropriate points.

I would like to express my gratitude to Denis Johnston for his kindness and cooperation in the preparation of this study. Whether in interview or correspondence, he was invariably considerate and helpful. I owe a special debt to my friend and colleague, Dr. Bernard Dick, who was always available for practical and much-needed advice and encouragement. My thanks also to the staff of the Reference Section and the Periodicals Section of the Fairleigh Dickinson University Library, Teaneck Campus, especially Mrs. Ruth Schwartz, Mrs. Mary McMahon, and Miss Marcia Lawlis, and to two kind ladies of the Peacham Library, Peacham, Vermont. Finally, I am forever grateful to my friends of many years, Dr. and Mrs. Charles L. Leavitt, who provided me with an ideal place in which to write most of this book.

GENE A. BARNETT

Fairleigh Dickinson University

Chronology

1901   William Denis Johnston born in Dublin, June 18.
1908–1915 Student at St. Andrew's College, Dublin.
1917–1918
1915–1916 Student at Merchiston Castle, Edinburg.
1919–1923 Christ's College, Cambridge University; wrote honors exams in history and law; B.A. and LL.B.
1922   Elected President of the Cambridge Union.
1923–1924 Harvard University Law School, Pugsley Scholar; student of Felix Frankfurter. A serious interest in theater dates from this year.
1925   Called to the Bar, Inner Temple, London, and King's Inns, Dublin.
1925–1929 Affiliated with the Dublin Drama League and the New Players, organizations loosely connected with the Abbey Theatre, Dublin.
1926   Christ's College, Cambridge, M.A. and LL.M.
1926   Called to the Bar, Northern Ireland.
1926   Submits the first draft of *The Old Lady Says "No!"* (then called *Shadowdance*) to the Abbey Theatre.
1928   Directs F. J. McCormick in the title role of *King Lear,* the first production of Shakespeare at the Abbey Theatre.
1928   Marriage, December 28, to Shelah Richards, Dublin; one son, Micheal, and one daughter, Jennifer.
1929   Premiere of *The Old Lady Says "No!"* at the Gate Theatre, Dublin, July 3.
1931–1936 On the Board of Directors of the Gate Theatre, Dublin.
1931   Premiere of *The Moon in the Yellow River,* Abbey Theatre, April 27.
1932   American premiere of *The Moon in the Yellow River,* New York City, February 29.
1933   Premiere of *A Bride for the Unicorn,* Gate Theatre, Dublin, May 9.
1934   Premiere of *Storm Song* at the Gate Theatre, Dublin, January 30.
1934   American premiere of *A Bride for the Unicorn,* Harvard Dramatic Club, Cambridge, Massachusetts, May 2.

1935	American premiere of *The Old Lady Says "No!,"* Amherst College, Amherst, Massachusetts, May 16.
1936	Premiere of *Blind Man's Buff,* an adaptation of Ernst Toller's *Die blinde Göttin* (1932), Abbey Theatre, December 28.
1936	Gives up law practice; joins BBC, Belfast.
1937–1939	Television producer for BBC, London.
1939	Premiere of *The Golden Cuckoo,* Gate Theatre, Dublin, April 25.
1939–1940	BBC, American Liaison Unit, London.
1940	Premiere of *The Dreaming Dust,* Gaiety Theatre, Dublin, March 25.
1940–1942	Writer, broadcaster, and director for BBC, London and Manchester.
1942–1945	War correspondent for BBC in the Middle East, Italy, France, and Germany.
1945	Awarded the Order of the British Empire.
1945	Divorced; marriage to Betty Chancellor, Dubin, March 25; two sons, Jeremy and Rory.
1946–1947	Director of Programs, BBC Television Service, London.
1947	Arranged and recorded for BBC-TV the only interview given by George Bernard Shaw on his ninetieth birthday at Ayot St. Lawrence.
1947–1949	Came to America and wrote for NBC's "Theater Guild on the Air"; various other scripting jobs for films and plays.
1948	His only one-act play, *A Fourth for Bridge.*
1950	Visiting Professor, Amherst College, spring semester.
1950	American premiere of *The Golden Cuckoo,* Provincetown, Massachusetts, August 17.
1950–1960	Professor of English, Mt. Holyoke College.
1953	*Nine Rivers from Jordan,* English edition.
1954	American premiere of *The Dreaming Dust,* Provincetown, Massachusetts, July 19.
1955	*Nine Rivers from Jordan,* American edition.
1955–1956	Guggenheim Fellowship for research on Swift.
1956	Premiere of *Strange Occurrence on Ireland's Eye,* Abbey Theatre, August 20.
1958	American premiere of *The Scythe and the Sunset,* Cambridge, Massachusetts, March 14; Irish premiere, Abbey Theatre, May 19.

1959   Libretto for the opera, *Six Characters in Search of an Author,* music by Hugo Weisgall, produced by the New York City Opera, Lincoln Center, April 26.

1959   *In Search of Swift* published in Dublin.

1960   A volume of collected plays, *The Old Lady Says "No!" and Other Plays,* published in England and America.

1960–1966 Chairman, Department of Theater, Smith College.

1965   *John Millington Synge,* "Columbia Essays on Modern Writers."

1966–1967 Visiting Professor, Amherst College.

1967–1968 Visiting Professor, University of Iowa.

1968   Libretto for the opera, *Nine Rivers from Jordan,* music by Hugo Weisgall, produced by the New York City Opera, Lincoln Center, October 9.

1968   *The Brazen Horn.*

1970–1971 Visiting Professor, University of California, Davis.

1971–1972 Visiting Professor, New York University.

1972–1973 Visiting Professor, Whitman College.

1973–   Living in Dalkey, County Dublin.

1977   Revival of *The Old Lady Says "No!,"* Abbey Theatre, Dublin, February 17.

1977   Publication of *Dramatic Works,* I.

CHAPTER 1

The Sow That Eats Her Farrow:
The Old Lady Says "No!"

I N the autumn of 1928, Dublin theatergoers could look forward
to two interesting and important opening nights. The Abbey
Theatre was planning its first production of a Shakespearean play,
King Lear, which was to be directed by Denis Johnston, age
twenty-seven and new to the Abbey in this particular capacity.
Although the company was well into its third decade, it had never
given Shakespeare, and it wanted to make a strong showing with
Lear in which the title role would be portrayed by one of its best
actors, F. J. McCormick. Nearby in the small Peacock Theatre,
two young actors, Micheal MacLiammoir and Hilton Edwards, one
Irish and the other English, were preparing a production of *Peer
Gynt* which was to introduce a new theater company, the Dublin
Gate, named and modeled after Peter Godfrey's London Gate
Theatre. These two theatrical ventures, seemingly unrelated, were,
in fact, of special significance in a series of events that led within a
few months to another opening night, the premiere of what has
been called with much justification "one of the best first plays ever
written": Denis Johnston's *The Old Lady Says "No!"*[1]

Why Johnston, young and relatively unknown to Dublin
audiences, was chosen to direct the Abbey's first Shakespeare is a
question with at least two answers, depending on whose version one
accepts. Of special interest is the more fully documented account —
and therefore the best known if not necessarily correct one —
because it furnishes the background for the genesis of *The Old
Lady Says "No!"* Quite simply, Lady Augusta Gregory, a founder
and one of the directors of the Abbey, felt W. B. Yeats offered the

15

job of directing *Lear* to Johnston as a consolation prize for not having accepted his first play for production. On October 29, 1928 she recounted in her journal her annoyance not only with the choice of the play ("I had never even been told it was being put on") but with the choice of director: "Denis Johnston ... has no connection with us, and I fancy it was given to him to make up for the rejection of his Emmet play."[2]

Her skepticism about Johnston's assignment was still discernible three weeks later when she "looked on" at a rehearsal and found it "rather inchoate at present," but four days later she looked in again and predicted it would "go very well." Her more positive feelings regarding the production were justified when *King Lear* opened the next day, November 26, 1928; she found it "wonderful, McCormick magnificent — there is no other word — all through." Apparently the director's approach pleased her, for she praised the staging and found it "wonderful that a play Queen Elizabeth had seen should still be so alive, so emotional," all of which reflected credit on Johnston whose share in the endeavor could hardly have been small.

In the meantime, she noted in her journal that Johnston had "spoken to Hilton Edwards, who will put on his Robert Emmet play, we [i.e., the Abbey Theatre] guaranteeing against loss up to £.50."[3] The "Emmet play" which had been rejected and was now being, in effect, subsidized by the theater that had turned it down was, of course, *The Old Lady*. And Lady Gregory assumed Yeats was trying to "make up" for this rejection by offering Johnston an opportunity to direct. There is another account with a different answer: Johnston himself, in a recent interview, denied Lady Gregory's version, saying simply that Yeats "got me to do some direction in the Abbey. And this wasn't, as people said, because he had turned down *The Old Lady Says "No!"*[4]

The affair involving *The Old Lady* began in 1926 when Johnston submitted to the Abbey Theatre a short Expressionistic play called *Shadowdance*. Expressionism in drama generally involves an emotional, highly subjective presentation of reality through symbolism and abstractions. As a theatrical way of life, it was not a style with which the Abbey felt completely comfortable, so W. B. Yeats, who was interested in if not always sympathetic to experimentation, had, with Lennox Robinson, given the backing of the Abbey and his own personal prestige to the founding of the Dublin Drama League which, in the years following its institution in 1918, had presented chiefly non-Irish plays of an experimental nature, many Expressionistic in style, works by August Strindberg, Luigi Pirandello, Georg Kaiser, Ernst Toller, and Eugene O'Neill. In fact, the League's production of *The Emperor Jones* had been taken over for a run by the parent company early in 1927 and constituted, in the words of a recent critic, "the first true invasion of the modern into the national theatre."[5]

Yet, a little more than a year after the O'Neill production, Sean O'Casey had submitted *The Silver Tassie* with its Expressionistic second act to the Abbey Board of Directors, and though there were some misgivings about doing so, they had turned it down. Johnston's *Shadowdance* had been read by Yeats in 1926 and found unsatisfactory. The young barrister-playwright revised the play several times and resubmitted it as *Symphony in Green*,[6] but it still could not garner enough support among the directors. It simply was not the kind of play the Abbey preferred to produce. Over thirty years later, Johnston admitted that both his play and O'Casey's *Tassie* were "of a type quite outside the competence of the Abbey's Directors at that time."[7] His script was eventually returned to him with the words "The old lady says no" written on a sheet of paper attached to the play:

Whether it was intended to inform me that the play had been rejected or whether it was being offered as an alternative to my own coy little name for the play — *Shadowdance* — is a question that I never liked to ask. But it remained, thereafter, as the title of the work — a definite improvement for which I have always been grateful. Lennox Robinson used to complain bitterly about any suggestion that Lady G. was against the play, but all I know of the matter is the distaste she expressed to me in the back sitting-room of her hotel in Harcourt Street.[8]

Almost certainly Augusta Gregory was "the old lady" in question here; this sobriquet was sometimes applied to her by the less reverential members of the theater company. And while the Abbey was not willing to produce the play, it was, as she noted in her journal, willing to risk fifty pounds on it if the Gate Theatre wished to undertake it.

The Gate indeed wished to undertake it; it was exactly the kind of play — Irish or otherwise — they wanted. This new company headed by MacLiammoir and Edwards had opened its first season with Henrik Ibsen's *Peer Gynt* at the small Peacock Theatre in October, 1928, and proceeded with a schedule of new experimental plays and classics from abroad that had received scant attention in Ireland. The first season had included, for example, O'Neill's Expressionistic *The Hairy Ape* as well as *Anna Christie,* and the second season listed another example of American Expressionism, Elmer Rice's *The Adding Machine.* At this point, in the spring of 1929, the rejected *Old Lady* arrived, and no play could have had a warmer welcome from producers. MacLiammoir himself took the central role of Robert Emmet, and for him it remained "the most musically exhilarating experience I have had on the stage."[9]

Recently in an interview, MacLiammoir recalled that his most satisfying experience as an actor, second only to nine productions of *Hamlet,* was his role in "a strange play called *The Old Lady Says* " 'No!' "[10] Hilton Edwards contributed distinguished direction to what was, as Johnston said, "a director's play, written very much in the spirit of 'Let's see what would happen if we did this or that.' "[11] It must all have been a nearly ideal experience for a young dramatist with his first production. Recently Johnston remarked that *The Old Lady* "got that rare thing in the theatre — a combination of a dramatist, a director, and an actor, each of them contributing something in his own field.... Everything that each added suited the others — a curious kind of situation. Ever since then we've always tried to reproduce that original production as closely as possible."[12]

In 1929, only a few years after the disruptions of O'Casey's *The Plough and the Stars,* difficulties and even vociferous objections might have been expected on opening a play like *The Old Lady.* Johnston himself admits it is "my only work that might fairly be described as anti-Irish."[13] The Dublin audience did make some attempt to live up to its reputation, for MacLiammoir records that, along with the "thunders of applause," there was abuse and the "usual accusations that the author had 'flung mud and dirt at the Irish people.' "[14] However, the play had an extended run — it was the final play of the season — and the theater was fully booked. Since that premiere, vehement dissenters have generally been in the minority, while the play's reputation as a modern, if not very well known, classic has grown.

The narrative thread of *The Old Lady Says "No!"* may be very simply and briefly stated: an actor playing the role of the great Irish patriot, Robert Emmet, in an old-fashioned historical melodrama is accidentally stunned during a performance. While he is unconscious, he has a dream in which he thinks he *is* Emmet, a dream that is a nightmare in which he searches compulsively for his lost love, Sarah Curran, in a modern Dublin he can hardly recognize, in an Ireland no longer sympathetic to his idealistic vision of what his country should be. The body of the play dramatizes the frustration of Emmet at the difference between his romantic dream of a free Ireland and the unheroic realities of the early years of the modern Irish Free State. However, a brief summary of the main plot line can hardly convey the subtlety and complexity of *The Old Lady*. Before further analysis, certain aspects should be briefly considered. Almost from the first, serious critical evaluation of the play has generally focused on three areas: its satire, obscurity, and Expressionistic technique.

II   *The Playwright as Satirist*

Una Ellis-Fermor, perhaps the soundest historian of the Irish dramatic movement, thought *The Old Lady* to be "a satiric review of certain dominant elements in Irish life, thought, political history and literature, and an acute exposure of the sentimentality that may be inherent in some of them."[15] More recently, Vivian Mercier, after remarking that "the most striking single fact about Irish literature in either Gaelic or English is the high proportion of satire which it contains," concludes that, with one minor exception, Johnston's *Old Lady* is "the only work by an Abbey Theatre dramatist . . . which is integrally conceived as a satire."[16]

Certainly not many public icons are left unscathed in this play: patriotism, sentimentality, political idealism, native puritanism, cultural pretensions, provinciality, romanticized history, melodramatic theater, and other general clichés of Irish life. More particular and personal targets are also subtly skewered: O'Casey's manners and his urban dialogue, Synge's poetic rural speech, Yeats' idealization of Cathleen Ni Houlihan, the ballads of Thomas Moore and other Irish poets, Robert Emmet as the prototypical Irish rebel, the rhetoric of Irish political speeches, the theatrical death scene, peasant heroines, censorship of the arts, and child performers. Also contributing to the total satiric effects of the play is the structure, which contrasts dream sequences with a prologue and epilogue that are concerned with presenting realistically an old-fashioned melodrama in "performance" before an audience in a theater.

III *The Charge of Obscurity*

The Old Lady Says "No!" is almost always described as a difficult and demanding play. Johnston himself has acknowledged "some occasional chaff about obscurity." This charge might have been made in reference to the Expressionistic technique the playwright employed, but probably this is not the case. Rather, it is what John Jordan refers to as "its weight of allusion"; the play has "all the marks of a brilliant young man's eclectic reading."[17] The range is from the Bible down through James Joyce, with a heavy dependence, in the first few pages, on minor Irish poets of the eighteenth and nineteenth centuries. Curtis Canfield, who did the first important criticism of Johnston's work, did not even bother to discuss such obscure allusions: he simply made an appendix of titles and authors quoted or paraphrased in the first scene of the play (approximately the first four pages). There are forty-three entries.[18]

It has been suggested that a speech without at least one quotation or reference is exceptional; however, Johnston himself commented recently that "there is less 'quotation' in the whole play than is usually assumed."[19] It is certainly true that "each allusion has a thematic point usually dependent upon the premise that the audience is Dublin Irish."[20] Paradoxically, this very quality that makes the play difficult also makes it extremely rich in texture, inviting to study, and exciting to read or see. Lacking this heavy use of allusion, it would be an entirely different and, one suspects, a less great play. Johnston has admitted that *The Old Lady* " 'to be intelligible to a non-Irish audience requires to some extent to be translated.' "[21] The point of the play may be fully appreciated only in Dublin, for it is "not quite the same play in London or New York."[22] Hilton Edwards finds its obscurity merely a "hall-mark of its period," the 1920s, when audiences were given credit for more intelligence than they possessed.[23] Robert Hogan thinks it is "one of the few plays to use allusion as thickly as does modern poetry" and finds its demands unusual but no more so than the demands of work by T. S. Eliot and Ezra Pound whose poetry offered similar challenges at about the same time.[24]

IV *The Expressionistic Form*

Perhaps more important than the use of allusion, reference, and quotation is the Expressionistic form of *The Old Lady*. Canfield

discussed the dramatist's use of Expressionistic devices and techniques in a long note which introduced the play in its first American
edition (1936). He focused primarily on the work as a dream play *à
la* August Strindberg with no barriers of time, space, and action
and no recognition of "logical causation, inevitable effects, and
responsible sequences."[25] The symbolic characters, the contra-
puntal arrangement of speeches and scenes, the repetition of certain words and phrases, the sets which melt into one another for
quick scene shifts, and the rhythmic contrasts in dialogue — these
are the principal techniques on which the play depends. Johnston
himself referred to *The Old Lady* as "an expressionistic gesture of
dissent" and insisted that at the time of its composition, it was "a
fairly original type of play" which technically owed less to other
dramatists than anything that he has since written.[26]

It was, in fact, a highly original play to come out of Ireland at
that time, and Johnston was probably the only Irish playwright
who could have written a completely Expressionistic work for the
theater in the Twenties. Certainly his is the first. In commenting on
the play, he has attempted to play down the influence of the
Expressionists as well as other "experimental" writers of the era
such as O'Neill and James Joyce who, he said, did not have much
to do with *The Old Lady*. The true "foster parents," he claims, are
two plays not often produced now, Josef Capek's *The Land of
Many Names* and George Kaufman and Marc Connelly's comedy
Beggar on Horseback.[27]

Capek's play was translated and published in London in 1926.[28]
Briefly, it is the story of a sick urban society's search for an ideal
land, a Utopia, which appears suddenly as a new continent, caused
by an earthquake, in the middle of the ocean. After attempts at
economic exploitation of the new land result in a war, a second
quake causes it to sink back into the sea. Because it represented the
various dreams of a better future for many people in that society,
the new continent came to be known as "the land of many names."
The moral seems to be drawn by Pieris, a poet, who tells the crowd
that the Old World where they live, not the idealized new continent,
is the true land of redemption in which their dreams can be fulfilled
through honest and sustained effort, and not through exploitation
and sudden riches.

Of the two "foster parents," Capek's work is the more interesting, and although dated now, its central situation, theatricality, and
satiric thrust offer some fairly obvious parallels with Johnston's

play. For example, the romantic search for an ideal land that is all things to all men is the search of Johnston's Robert Emmet for a romantic, idealized Ireland in *The Old Lady.* In Johnston's play, the "many names" are there as a series of allusions that suggest various levels on which to approach the idea of the search: Hy Brasail (paradise), Tir-Na-n'Og (land of eternal youth), the Land of Heart's Desire, the New Jerusalem, Eden, the Dublin of the future, a free Ireland, and even Rathfarnham, the village of the Priory where Sarah Curran lives. Capek's various types of characters — most with names that are merely labels — are like the Dubliners in *The Old Lady,* and Johnston's Blind Fiddler, although a stock figure in Irish literature, is reminiscent of Capek's poet, Pieris. The urban settings of both plays constantly shift for brief scenes, and both plays make striking use of chairoscuro. Even the dialogue of Capek's play is echoed occasionally in *The Old Lady.*

The Kaufman and Connelly comedy of 1924, *Beggar on Horseback,* is a period piece that holds up only moderately well, as a major production in New York's Lincoln Center demonstrated in 1970. The play teaches with the simplicity of a parable that art and big business do not mix. A young composer, poor but talented, neglects his work on a symphony in order to support himself by doing orchestrations of popular music. He is about to be swallowed up by a vulgar, *nouveau riche* family as a husband for their fickle daughter, a match that would destroy his creativity. In a fantastic dream that takes up much of the two-act play, he has a revelation of what marriage with the rich girl would be like with its constant emphasis on money, its total insensitivity to his music, and its round of empty social activities. At the end of the play, he is rewarded with a nice-girl-next-door who will love him and nurture his talent so they may live happily and artistically ever after. Their American Dream is complete except for money, but that is partly the point of a play that is a satirical attack on America's reverence for the dollar.

Johnston thought the work "a superb piece of American expressionism."[29] For its time, the play did make brilliant use of certain devices that influenced Johnston in *The Old Lady,* most notably the dream sequence which is framed by realistic scenes, much as Emmet's dream-journey through the nightmare world of modern Dublin is framed by scenes of an old melodrama in performance. In addition, this American comedy is surprisingly clever in its varied use of music for contrast, humor, irony, and satire. For example, jazz is heard occasionally throughout the play as a contrast to the more classically structured music in which the young composer is interested.

Another device the two plays have in common is the fusion of realistic characters into similar or even quite different counterparts in the dream sequences. Sets too flow into one another without any break as the plays move easily and swiftly from one scene to another. In both plays several simultaneous conversations suggest the distressing cacophony of modern urban life, while some speeches are composed only of fragments jumbled together. Finally, there is the basic motivation for both main characters: as the young musician searches for a chance at artistic fulfillment, Robert Emmet searches for the lost spirit of revolution and Sarah Curran. *Beggar on Horseback* was indeed richly suggestive to Johnston when he came to write his first play.

V *An Irish* Dream Play

The structure of *The Old Lady* is one of its most interesting features and may be considered from several angles, but however the play is viewed, it is always apparent that it works because of the latitude Expressionism permits. First, there is the device of the dreamer and his dream for which August Strindberg set the pattern in *A Dream Play* (1902). In Strindberg's play, Indra's daughter comes to earth to experience the life of mortals, finds life too tragic to be sustained, and returns to her father in another realm. Similarly, Robert Emmet — or the actor, called the Speaker, who is supposed to be performing the role of Emmet — finds that he has left the dream world of a play set in 1803 and entered the garish world of Dublin of the 1920s. At the play's conclusion, Emmet's dream ends, and the real audience is returned to the "reality" of the melodrama, as a doctor comes from the wings with a rug to cover the still unconscious actor.

Almost equally obvious is the play-within-a-play technique, the classic example of which is Luigi Pirandello's *Six Characters in Search of an Author* which also explores the illusion-reality theme in the context of a theatrical performance. Perhaps what is unique in *The Old Lady* is the scene that functions as a prologue. The old nineteenth-century melodrama that the audience is watching as the play begins is, first of all, a parody of a type of play once common on the Irish stage; second, it is a pastiche of quotations and paraphrasings of Irish poets and balladeers; third, it is a highly idealized episode in Irish history. This prologue also satirizes the very stuff of which it is made and a good deal else, while establishing a mood which will stand in strong contrast to the more pungent satire and the frenzied pace of the rest of the play.

The most valid approach to the structure of *The Old Lady* may be made through the clue in the descriptive phrase which Johnston has placed under the title: "A Romantic Play in Two Parts with Choral Interludes." The last two words suggest that the play might be compared to a long musical composition in two main movements which are interrupted and embellished throughout with choral sections chanted, sung, or spoken. The old melodrama functions as an introduction to these two movements. The structure of the rest of the play depends not on a linear narrative line but on an unsystematic arrangement of themes and leitmotifs which, as in music, recur throughout. "To understand it," says Curtis Canfield, "we must first forget Scribe and remember Beethoven...."[30]

To sustain the simple plot of *The Old Lady,* the playwright constructs a series of episodes — or, as Constantine Curran called them, "epiphanies of Dublin life" —[31] which are only very loosely related to the events of Robert Emmet's search for Sarah Curran. These episodes function as short musical movements within the two main divisions.

The play opens with a romantic prologue like a melodic overture which falsely lulls the audience into easy expectations which the author has no intention of fulfilling. (Johnston speaks with amusement of how, at a number of early performances before the word got around, some in the audience were taken in by the call for a doctor for the "injured" actor, and concerned physicians offered their services on stage.)[32] This prologue is in the tradition of nineteenth-century romantic opera, and it is worth mentioning that one of the questions the author and producers wanted to answer with their first production was whether an opera could be constructed that did not have to be sung.[33] The prologue-overture establishes the romantic major theme of the search for Sarah Curran, but it also introduces a series of leitmotifs through quotations and allusions which, as they recur throughout the play, contrast ironically with the prologue.

What follows this introductory movement, Canfield describes as a "two-part Nocturn," made up of a series of encounters with Dubliners, Part One of which climaxes with the shooting of Joe, a bystander who is part-patriot and part-poet and who symbolizes the best in Irish youth.[34] Part Two is introduced by the "grotesque cadenza" of the pretentious artistic gathering in a "fantastically respectable drawing-room," a cadenza which gradually resolves into two minor themes: the transmogrification of Sarah into the old Flower Woman and the death of Joe. The play concludes with the dance of the shadows of Dublin's great that gave the play its original title, *Shadowdance*.

VI   *The Loom of History*

Johnston once wrote that all of his plays in the collected edition were historical with one exception. *The Old Lady* is probably more dependent on a historical background than any of these excepting only *The Dreaming Dust*. Robert Emmet was such a popular subject in the nineteenth century poetry and theater of Ireland that it is possible to speak of "a tradition of Emmet plays."[35] In the twentieth century, at least two other notable Irish dramatists turned to this strikingly romantic historical figure as a subject for the theater: Lennox Robinson with *The Dreamers* (1915) and Paul Vincent Carroll with *The Conspirators* (also called *The Coggerers*, 1934). Johnston's play is, on one level, "a satire of the Emmet legend"; on another, it is "an organic continuation of that legend into the disillusioned 1920s."[36]

Emmet's story is commonplace mythology in Ireland, for in addition to its chauvinistic appeal, it has all the right ingredients of nineteenth-century romance. Born in 1778, Emmet came from a Protestant family with strong nationalistic leanings. After becoming a leader of the United Irishmen, he led an unsuccessful uprising in Dublin in July, 1803. Emmet managed to escape to the mountains, but on one of his clandestine visits to Dublin to see Sarah Curran, the daughter of John Philpot Curran, an eminent advocate, he was captured by Major Henry Sirr, an Englishman, who became the villain in all Irish accounts of the affair. Before Emmet was hanged and beheaded on September 20 of that year, he delivered at the Session House in Dublin — before the court which had just convicted him of treason — an impromptu speech that is still stirring and has become one of the gems of Irish oratory. His defense against the charge of treason concludes with the famous passage that begins "Let no man write my epitaph," lines on which Johnston drew for the conclusion of *The Old Lady*. Two years later, Sarah Curran married a British officer and a few months later died in Sicily of a broken heart, as the Irish prefer to think. The only immediate effect of the uprising was the murder by Emmet's followers of one of the most compassionate British judges in Ireland, Arthur Wolfe, Lord Kilwarden.

Emmet's story is one of those episodes in history with "that delightful quality of story-book unreality that creates a glow of satisfaction without any particular reference to the facts of life."[37] Nor is Johnston interested in setting the facts straight in his "history" play, for he is not concerned with Emmet except as a "generic patriot" who therefore may speak not only his own historic words but also those of other Irish political heroes such as Charles Stewart Parnell and Patrick Henry Pearse, and the chauvinist lines of the more romantic poets such as James Mangan and Thomas Moore.[38] But it is exactly this kind of patriot who may, with the highest of motives, blindly sacrifice himself, his cause, and his country's peace by resorting to violence to effect political change. In time, his romantic patriotism will become part of the national myth and so furnish additional inspiration to others like him without, as Johnston wrote, "any particular reference to the facts."

Both admirable and destructive, this romantic patriotism of the past that can so easily be self-perpetuating is one aspect of Johnston's main theme, but as Robert Hogan points out, such nationalistic idealism is contrasted with "a modern sentimentalizing of that ideal and with an even more modern emptiness of spirit."[39] To put it another way, Johnston is juxtaposing "the dismal reality of the Irish situation in the twenties — revolt, civil war, assassination, atrocities — against the rage for sentiment — religious, political, cultural, emotional — which is precisely the source of self-perpetuating violence."[40] This is the main theme of *The Old Lady*.

VII   *Bluster and Ballads*

The prologue or overture to the two main movements of the drama is the playlet, lasting about ten minutes, that performs several functions in the work as a whole. It establishes the love affair and the forcible separation of the lovers, which in turn leads to the archetypal quest of the lover for his beloved. It is this plot device that transforms an old-fashioned, melodramatic style of playwriting into a modern, almost Expressionistic method of characterization through dialogue by showing Robert Emmet and Sarah, not as real people, but as the romantic lover/national hero attended by his faithful, loving Irish sweetheart. In addition, the whole romantic tone and mood of this episode stand in direct contrast to the rest of the play, for sharp contrast in tone, lighting, dialogue, and character is a structural principle throughout. Further, the prologue establishes through the use of songs and poetry as dialogue certain verbal leitmotifs which recur throughout the play and function satirically in the scenes set in modern Dublin. Since this is the most important function of these quotations, a detailed consideration of two examples will give some indication of the multiplicity of meaning they contribute to the play as a whole.

The play opens on an almost dark stage with "The Shan Van Vocht," a famous patriotic ballad, sung in the distance. A Dublin audience would certainly associate this song with the earlier unsuccessful Uprising of 1798 (thus implicitly commenting on Emmet's own undertaking only five years later). Lord Edward Fitzgerald, prominent in the earlier revolt, had been trapped by Major Sirr, the "jackel of the Pale" in the song and the same officer who subsequently captured Robert Emmet. The imminent arrival of the "villain" on the scene is thus foreshadowed, as well as the capture and death of a new national hero and martyr. "The Shan Van Vocht" means "the Poor Old Woman" and symbolizes, like Cathleen Ni Houlihan, Ireland herself, thus subtly announcing the title of the play. Further, the opening ballad heralds the entry a few minutes later of "the old tattered Flower Woman," the wheezing old hag who represents the Ireland of the Twenties, "the old sow that eats her farrow," as Joyce called her. This old crone innocently appears like some ancient Eliza Doolittle ("Penny a bunch th' violets") at the foot of Henry Grattan's statue facing College Green. Her second line in the play ("Me four bewtyful gre-in fields") would indicate to an Irish audience that she is a perversion and parody of Yeats' Cathleen Ni Houlihan (who has the same line — but without the wonderfully low-class Irish accent — in his play of that title) and so a different and slightly disreputable version of the Shan Van Vocht.

This transmogrification of Yeats' respectable old beldame into Johnston's spiteful witch who begs under the guise of selling apples and flowers is carefully developed in lines that strongly echo *Cathleen Ni Houlihan,* such as "God bless ye, lovely gentleman, spare a copper for a cuppa tea. Spare a copper for yer owin old lady, for when th' trouble is on me I must be talkin' te me friends."[41]

Compare Yeats' *Cathleen* in which the Old Woman's first line is "God save all here!" and later: "Sometimes my feet are tired and my hands are quiet, but there is no quiet in my heart. When the people see me quiet, they think old age has come on me and that all the stir has gone out of me. But when the trouble is on me I must be talking to my friends."

The vitality of Johnston's dialogue derives from the old Flower Woman's colorful, low-class accent, the contrast with Grattan's and the Speaker's more refined speech, and the parody of Yeats's *Cathleen*. Later, Johnston's old Flower Woman is merged with the characters of Sarah Curran. Thus there is an ambiguity regarding the object of Emmet's search: Ireland is both a railing old witch and a beautiful young lady. This paradox is basic to the play, and its origin is to be found in the opening ballad, "The Shan Van Vocht," which, it should be noted, is heard one last time during the Speaker's monologue which is the last speech of the play.

According to Canfield's appendix, Johnston drew on a total of thrity-eight different poems or songs in the opening scene, and Thomas Moore, Dublin-born poet and patriot (1779–1852), wrote four of them. Sarah Curran's first words to Emmet ("I think, oh my love, 'tis they voice from the kingdom of souls!") are from Moore's "At the Mid Hour of Night," which ironically is a lament for a dead lover that now in Sarah's mouth becomes a premonition of his death. Later, Emmet questions her with a line from Moore's "When He Who Adores Thee": "When he who adores thee has left but a name, ah say, wilt thou weep?" Aside from the humor in the stilted form of this somewhat morbid question, there is the added irony that we already know the answer, an answer which she indeed gives in her reply, which is also from Moore but from another poem ("O, Breathe Not His Name"): "I shall not weep, I shall not breathe his name." Then she adds from yet another Moore poem ("She Is Far From the Land"), "For my heart in his grave will be lying." "And lying," Johnston notes, considering Sarah's actions after Emmet's death, "is the operative word."

This romantic little ballad is, more than any other, a satiric theme song for the play, for it is sung *in toto* by the General in the drawing room scene early in Part Two. At that point in the play, it is clearly meant to satirize not only the "story-book" love of

Emmet and Sarah but the cliché the ballad has itself become.

This marvelous scene set in a "fantastically respectable drawing-room" is probably one of the most entertaining to watch and one of the most challenging to stage effectively. Structurally, the final portion of the scene is one of the most accomplished examples of the use of contrast in the play. The Speaker/Actor, now dazed from the blow on his head, begins with poetic dialogue from the opening moments of the play. Some of the lines he speaks were originally Sarah's; the point is that he knows all the lines of the play but cannot recall which are his own and which are hers. As the General sings Moore's ballad, the Minister and O'Cooney reminisce about the days of the Troubles, O'Rooney both shocks and amuses with his speech about virginity, and O'Mooney explains Saint Peetric, a quip Johnston had unknowingly borrowed from Joyce's *Finnegans Wake.*

What Johnston is doing here is worth noting carefully, for it has an extra dimension afforded by the present warfare in North Ireland. Running in counterpoint to the General's vocalizing about Sarah's undying faithfulness and the Speaker's patriotic exhortation to awake and be blest are satiric comments on three of Ireland's most sacred conceits: reverence for Saint Peter and Saint Patrick and the purity of Irish womanhood. In Synge's time this would have caused rioting. The coda to this scene comes when O'Cooney (a satiric portrait of Sean O'Casey) speaks with sentimental longing for the days of the Troubles: "And that night waiting up on the North Circular for word of the executions. Ah, not for all the wealth of the world would I give up the maddenin' minglin' memories of the past..." (65).

The speech is almost black humor, in addition to being a parody of the kind of dialogue O'Casey wrote for Captain Jack in *Juno and the Paycock;* it also parallels the romantic attitude toward revolt which the Speaker and the General (by now in the third stanza of Moore's ballad) are simultaneously promoting. Finally, this scene not only evokes the hollow men on Dublin streets in the 1920s but, in a somewhat different way, the horrible reality of guerrilla warfare in present-day Ireland which is itself merely another episode in a long chain of political events that go back to the fifteenth century. Implicit in O'Cooney's lines is the warning: the Irish, in romanticizing their past deeds of civil violence, are blindly encouraging future martyrs of Emmet's type.

This scene concludes with more simultaneous speech and song as the Speaker blends phrases from Sir Aubrey DeVere ("Plorans Ploravit") and William Drennan ("Eire") with O'Cooney's parody of O'Casey, while the General, now down to the last stanza of Moore's "She Is Far From the Land," implores a grave for Sarah. As the Speaker joins in on the last lines of the ballad, both men conclude with a hopeful plea for "a glorious morrow" — a plea that ironically carries little hope of fulfillment, coming from these two.

Like most of the allusions and quotations in the prologue, these lines from Moore are clearly operative on several levels: to fore-shadow dramatically Emmet's death; to characterize with irony the depth of Sarah's affection for Emmet; to satirize the popular view of the famous lovers by undercutting it with emphasis on the near-pun on "lying"; to satirize Moore's ballad as national cliché by having the General sing it to a crude piano accompaniment while so much else goes on; and to comment critically on the unfounded optimism of a "glorious morrow" when "the State supports the Artist" and "the Artist supports the State" in a "small Art Saloon" where Gaelic is spoken and everything is "very nice nice nice."

The theatrically romantic mood of the first scene is shattered by the blow to Emmet's head, and a pseudo-reality reigns in the interval before the Speaker initiates the dream sequence. The only indication of anything unusual is the barely discernible movement of some dim figures behind a black gauze curtain. The contrast of light and dark is significant here, for the lights slowly come up on the scene of the delirious Speaker, and the dim shadows, now a chorus of "Forms," begin the first "choral interlude" with a whispered chant, first of names, then of words and phrases which do not make much sense but suggest the raucous complexity of urban Dublin in comparison to the tranquility of Rathfarnham.

Although *The Old Lady* was in some kind of completed form before O'Neill's *The Emperor Jones* had been presented by the Dublin Drama League late in 1926, it seems highly likely that John-ston's shadows which metamorphose into Forms owe a good deal to the "Little Formless Fears" that torment Brutus Jones in O'Neill's play. The "dim and distant boom-boom" of the drum suggests the pulse of a man under stress, much as the native drum-ming did in *Jones,* and the pulsing lights symbolize the mind gradu-ally coming back to consciousness through folds of darkness. This brief section builds to a cacophony of sounds amid the bright lights of Dublin which are a striking contrast to the quiet darkness of the first moments of the play. The tension of the Speaker is reflected in the climax of this brief scene with his line from James Mangan's "Dark Rosaleen" ("Red lightning tightening through my blood") already quoted in the prologue.

VIII   *Part One: "Dear Dirty Dublin"*

As the black gauze curtain parts (perhaps symbolizing the Speaker's complete breakthrough to the conscious "reality" of his dream-Dublin), the first of a series of short movements establishes through a brief scene with a stagehand the motif of the search for Sarah and for Rathfarnham, the romantic Ireland of the past, which is the main thread of the plot. There are two important scenes in the remainder of Part One: the Speaker's encounter with Grattan's statue and with the old Flower Woman, and the scene at the end when the old Flower Woman betrays the Speaker to the crowd he has just won over, thus leading to his shooting Joe.

At the stop for the Rathfarnham bus, the Speaker discovers there is no room, and he will have to wait for the next. This affords an opportunity for a debate with the nearby statue on the wisdom of Emmet's way to a new free Ireland as opposed to Grattan's way, with the dissolute Cathleen Ni Houlihan, the old Flower Woman, as ironic chorus commenting satirically on and to them both.

Henry Grattan (1746–1820) was an Irish statesman who is given chief credit for the restoration of independence to the Irish Parliament in 1782. Conveniently, his statue stands in front of College Green in Dublin facing one of the busiest traffic arteries. In terms of meaning, this is one of the key scenes of the play. Grattan's statue, it should be noted, has the features and voice of the British Major Sirr, Emmet's captor. Canfield is probably right in suggesting that Johnston was depending on this physical similarity not only to bridge the gap between the prologue and the play but also, and more importantly, to establish that Grattan and Major Sirr both stand in the same relationship to Emmet: both symbolize the opposition.[42]

Sirr, of course, is British authority in Ireland, and Grattan is a symbol of reason and mature wisdom brought to bear in Anglo-Irish politics, a striking contrast to Emmet's revolt. Grattan's first line, "How long, O Lord, how long?" is the curtain line of Shaw's *St. Joan.* The meaning is clear: "When will Ireland be receptive to the wisdom of a resolution through lawful means instead of violent rebellion?'' For men like Grattan, Ireland has become a stifling place: "The thick, sententious atmosphere of this little hell of babbling torment" chokes him. It was Emmet's patriotic "play-acting" that resulted in the pointless death of the compassionate judge, Kilwarden, although Emmet insists that he did his best to save him: "What more could I do.... It was horrible. But it was war" (34).

That such romantic idealism leads to violence and death is underscored later in Part One with these same words; after the speaker has shot Joe he demands of the onlookers, ''...what could I do? It was war'' (51). Grattan is still the rejected one here, an old man whose wise judgment is passed over for immediate and foolish action. Clearly he speaks for the author in urging a resolution to Ireland's troubles through wisdom and diplomacy: "Oh, it is an easy thing to draw a sword and raise a barricade. It saves working, it saves waiting. It saves everything but blood! And blood is the cheapest thing the good God has made" (34–35). (The old Flower Woman echoes these words when she demands her rights in the climax of this scene when Joe is shot by the Speaker.) The key speech here and perhaps the most significant in the play is Grattan's indictment of his countrymen's love affair with violence: "Ah, the love of death, creeping like a mist at the heels of my countrymen! Death is the only art in which we own no masters. Death is the only voice that can be heard in this distressful land where no man's word is taken, no man's message heeded, no man's prayer answered except it be his epitaph" (35).

The Speaker comes off second best in his argument with Grattan and cannot remember his lines, but there is still Rathfarnham: "They will understand there." Grattan has the last word; as the old Flower Woman sings a comic ballad, he scathingly sums up the point he has been making: "In my day Dublin was the second city of a mighty Empire. What is she now?" He scornfully answers his own question: "Free!" (36). But the Speaker, blind to the tragedy such efforts as his have caused, rejects Grattan's sentiments: "You are lying! ... Ghosts out of Hell, that's what you are" (37). As the black curtain falls and entraps him in its folds (suggesting his effort to blot out Grattan's truth), an old blind fiddler passes across the stage. Throughout this debate, the old Flower Woman has made ironic comments with snatches of song, offers of sale, and quotations from Yeats' *Cathleen Ni Houlihan* which sound strange on her lips.

The two brief scenes of the Flapper and the Medical (student) and the Well-dressed Woman and Businessman are, first, moments of relief in contrast with the more serious matters of the Grattan-Emmet scene. The chatter of the Flapper is semisophisticated and a pure delight. If she is empty-headed, the Trinity medical student is not much better off. Both are representative of the luckier half of Dublin youth, and the Well-dressed Woman and the Businessman are simply their counterparts fifteen to twenty years later. The Two Young Things converse in lower-class accents of matters that never rise above the *True Romances* level and are slightly flattered, if determined to appear otherwise, when the Speaker accosts them in his search for the bus to Rathfarnham. The minor fuss that ensues leads into the second important scene in Part One as the Speaker gains acceptance with the sidewalk crowd and an opportunity to address them. He is introduced by a long-winded Older Man who, at the moment of introduction, gets his name wrong, a name which has been "a household word wherever th' ole flag flies."

The Speaker's address to the crowd as he woos them with romantic patriotism comes in part from Patrick Pearse's speech at the O'Donovan Rossa Commemoration in 1915. Like Emmet's Dock Speech, it is a justly famous piece of Gaelic oratory, and it is still highly effective in the play. To the strains of "The Shan Van Vocht," it attracts followers to Emmet's banner, as the crowd shouts "Rathfarnham!" Clearly that is where the Speaker hopes to find Sarah, his idealized Cathleen. Since this is what the crowd wants (or thinks it wants), Rathfarnham becomes a symbolic Mecca for emotional Irish patriots: a Tir-na-n'Og or Hy Brasail, a New Jerusalem or the Land of Heart's Desire.

But at this point the rowdy scene turns sour. The Old Flower Woman demands her rights. "It's not food or drink that I want. It's not silver that I want," she insists in the lines of Yeats' Cathleen. "What is it he called it? . . . the cheapest thing the good God has made. . . . That's all. For your own old lady" (46–47). When she is put off by the Speaker, she first demands ("Gimme me rights") and then threatens ("Me rights first . . . or I'll bloody well burst ye!") and then betrays him to the crowd: "Let me tell youse that fella's not all he says he is!" As they turn against him, his identity suddenly hinges on the crucial question: *"What's happened to your boots?"* (In the prologue, the Speaker's boots had been removed after he had been hit on the head, and carpet slippers had been placed on his feet.) The boots are here symbolic of the romantic hero and lover, and it is humorously ironic that the Speaker's identity rests on the mere trappings of the man — which, of course, is Johnston's point: a nation swayed by externals will, to its ruin, always reject a Grattan and follow an Emmet. The Speaker's explanation that his boots were taken when he was *playing* Robert Emmet leads to his final rejection by the crowd and at the same time continues the motif of "play-acting" that follows the character through the play.

The crowd's rejection of the Speaker is done in terms that recall the rejection by the Home Rule party of Charles Stewart Parnell in Committee Room 15 of the House of Commons in London in December, 1890 (Speaker: "Who is the master of this party?" Older Man: "Who is the mistress of this party?").[43] Parnell, who might in a few more years have brought about a peaceable separation from England, was defeated by Irish morality when a scandal ensued over his affair with a young woman, and his party rejected his leadership. This evocation of Parnell here would seem to align him more with Grattan than with Emmet and patriots like Pearse.

In the last minutes of the scene, there is a return to melodrama, although not in the style of the prologue, when the Speaker seizes a gun belonging to a young man (Joe) and, when threatened by the crowd, fires and mortally wounds him. The dialogue here is a parody of melodramatic death scenes in modern plays and films. It was pointed out earlier that the Speaker's defense here is the same words he had used to Grattan to defend the murder of Lord Kilwarden by Emmet's supporters. Somehow his tactics always lead to bloodshed and the lame excuse that war justifies it. He can only retreat to a heroic posture: "Shoot back then! It is war. Shoot! I can die too!" (52). The old Flower Woman appears in the last seconds of this hour of blood as a requiem is chanted; she has her rights once more. She has drunk the reviving blood of a victim and is young again, and when she speaks it is with the voice of Sarah Curran. The Cathleen that demands blood knows neither age, form, nor class. She is national symbol and flesh-devouring matriarch, but to the Speaker she is still his beloved Sarah — and he still pursues her.

IX   Part Two: "No City of the Living"

Part Two is composed of three short movements and the final "shadowdance." The first of these involves a drawing-room gathering of "nice" people at the home of the Minister for Arts and Crafts; the second centers on the Blind Fiddler who was introduced without dialogue earlier in Part One, and the third returns to the young man, Joe, who was shot by the Speaker. There is a strikingly abrupt shift in mood from the first drawing-room scene to the second and third movements which are less dramatic, less humorous. The conclusion is a return for a few seconds to the stunned actor lying on the stage, about to be covered with a rug by an attending physician. Not much ground is gained thematically in Part Two, for the Speaker who was left calling for Sarah as Part One concluded has, of course, not found her at play's end. Despite what he has seen and heard, he seems as committed as ever to his symbolic search. Probably Johnston's view of such a romantic idealist is better served by letting him go, as Canfield says, "unregenerate and unashamed, a slippered Dante baffled but unbowed in a Dublin Inferno."[44]

The first movement within Part Two has its own short prologue. Maeve, the untalented offspring of the Minister for Arts and Crafts, reads A. A. Milne's "The King's Breakfast" to the art-worshippers in her father's drawing room. The conversation here is a marvelous satire of the Dublin philistine and pseudo-intellectual. The Minister insists that Talent and Art will add up to national dignity but only if the former is deserving and paternally censored as necessary and the latter is government-inspected for purity and cleanliness. Art obviously belongs, as far as this group is concerned, in a small salon frequented by the nicest people. The only dissenting voices are the artists themselves — O'Cooney (O'Casey), O'Mooney (the portrait artist Paddy Touhy), and the novelist O'Rooney (Liam O'Flaherty), but they too do not escape Johnston's satire.

When the Speaker arrives on his quest for Rathfarnham, he is barely remembered; "The gentleman who is far from the land," recalls the Minister's wife, confusing Emmet with Sarah. The Speaker recognizes some of those present: the redcoat who struck him on the head in the prologue has metamorphosed into the General. Although the old Flower Woman is noticed by the Speaker, the others refuse to acknowledge her existence. So common and repulsive has the embodiment of the national spirit become that even the most superficial patriot will have nothing to do with her. Grattan greets the Speaker as Don Quixote Alighieri and Galahad, allusions, of course, to other heroic quests. Using dialogue from

the old melodrama, the Speaker competes for attention with the
General's rendition of "She Is Far From the Land," the Minister's
conversation with O'Cooney, and the cynical comments of
O'Rooney and O'Mooney. As the General concludes Moore's
ballad, the Speaker is still frenziedly repeating snatches of poetry
from the opening moments of the play, but he is drawn into singing
the last lines of the song himself. They are in this context ironic
comments on his own death and the future of Ireland. Suddenly, it
is all too much for him, and the symbolic curtain blots it out of his
mind.

The succeeding scene focuses on the Blind Fiddler whom Johnston described as a "standard Abbey character," the "image of a
gloomy Gael."[45] This old man announces himself as a descendant
of the King of Thomond which would place him in the family line
of Brian Boru, one of Ireland's first national heroes. Royal blood
he may have, but he speaks with the tongue of Synge's peasants.
Presumably he symbolizes heroic Ireland gone to unhealthy seed, a
blind maker of jigs and tunes who must live on the remains of the
dead past. Ironically, the Speaker is reduced to asking his way of
this old dark Fiddler who has recognized him as Emmet by his singing of "She Is Far From the Land." Poor Bob Emmet died for Ireland, recalls the Fiddler. "How can I have died for Ireland," wonders the Speaker. As though to explain, the Fiddler sings to him
"The Struggle is Over," and the Speaker himself joins in the
refrain: "Bold Robert Emmet, the darling of Erin, / Bold Robert
Emmet will die with a smile" (67-68). ("Ah, them are the songs.
Them are the songs," remarks the Blind Fiddler in a droll parody
of O'Casey's Joxer Daley.)

The Flapper and Trinity Medical return for a brief scene, but
they are older, a little wiser, and slightly condescending in their
sophistication. "What would the likes of you have to do with the
likes of them?" asks the Fiddler of the Speaker. "Coming and
going on the mailboat. And they thinking themselves the real ones
— the strong ones! I do have to laugh sometimes..." (69). If the
Fiddler is the spirit of romantic Irish heroism and knows his own
kind in Emmet, he still recognizes that they are both superior to the
Flapper and the Medical and others like them who are "blind and
drunk with the brave sight of their own eyes." Dublin in the
Twenties has proven no breeding ground for heroes. The dark Fiddler is another blind seer like Teiresias who sees clearly that "This is
no City of the Living: but of the Dark and the Dead" (perhaps an

echo of the first line of Yeats' "Sailing to Byzantium"). In general, he seems to speak for Johnston, although the dramatist can hardly approve of his romantic sentimentality.

When the lights come up on the third and final movement before the concluding "shadowdance," the peeling plaster of the walls of a dingy tenement sharply contrasts with the brightly lighted drawing-room setting at the opening of Part Two. Unexpectedly, this movement centers around Joe whom the Speaker wounded at the end of Part One. This final movement seems the weakest of the major scenes of the play. For one thing, Joe, whom Grattan calls the "symbol of Ireland's genius," is not particularly convincing in his symbolic role; the longer it takes him to die, the less interesting he becomes. For another thing, the extended argument between the young Republican and the less-involved older man who is satisfied simply with the "status q-oh" (partition and the Free State) is one of the less vital dialogues of the play, although it does work as counterpoint to the Speaker's conversation with the old Flower Woman.

For the second time, there is a dramatic reminder that Sarah is just one embodiment of Cathleen. On a dark stage, her voice calls out for Emmet, but as the lights go up for the last movement to begin, the Speaker finds he is clasping not Sarah but the old Flower Woman in his arms. The joke is on him, and he admits it. There follows a grotesque and rowdy love scene as the Speaker, thoroughly disillusioned to find what his idealization of Ireland has become, cynically pays court to the repulsive old crone:

> (Speaker:)   Kiss me, lovely Sarah Curran!
> (Woman:)   (archly) Ah, go on owā that! D'juver
>   hear the like!   (71)

The Speaker is inebriated with the despair of a man who finds that the virginal object of his deepest love is in reality a tainted whore. To indicate the utter degeneration of Irish romantic idealism, the old Flower Woman is not even above making an indecent offer: "Ay . . . are ye lookin' for a bit of sport tonight?" (74). At this point the dying Joe turns on his "mudher" ("Strumpet! Strumpet!"), and she curses him. Joe's death scene is a signal for the entry of the Blind Fiddler and the appropriate moment for the most damning indictment in the play which best sums up the author's attitude: ". . . this land belongs not to them that are on it, but to them that are under it" (76).

The mood of the scene has changed. The Speaker is conscience-stricken over his killing of Joe and struck by the Younger Man's charge that he is only "a bloody play-actor": "If you were a man and not satisfied with the state of things, you'd alter them for yourself" (74). ". . . I am only a play-actor," he confesses (the only time in the play except for the boots episode), "unless I dare to contradict the dead! Must I do that?" This is an important question, for it is the dilemma that confronts the now disillusioned Speaker, and its resolution constitutes Johnston's main thesis. "To contradict the dead," is, first of all, to agree with that worn-out shell of Irish heroism, the Blind Fiddler, that Ireland has in the past belonged "not to them that are on it, but to them that are under it." The ghosts of dead heroes and a romantic vision of history have ruled present thinking too long, and it must not be so in the future. Further, "to contradict" is to declare that Emmet's way of political change through violence is wrong and self-defeating; to acknowledge that heroes like Emmet are self-indulgent in "playing" at the political game of rebellion; and to admit that as the Speaker he is indeed "only a play-actor" unless as a man he tries to alter "the state of things" in a rational manner.

Refusal "to contradict the dead" is to acquiesce in the belief that Ireland belongs to the past and will be ruled by it in future; to maintain that Emmet's way to a proud Ireland, secure in her place among nations, must and will sometime succeed; to believe that the Emmets, rather than the Grattans, are the truly inspired leaders; and to insist that the dreaming Speaker really *is* "Bold Robert Emmet." This question of daring to contradict crystallizes the dilemma; this is the Speaker's last line until he returns at the end of the "shadowdance" to "justify" the answer he will give.

Maeve appears to play a musical introduction ("The Struggle Is Over") as the complete cast, symbolizing a mourning Ireland, gathers for the wake which will become the dance of the shadows. The General wants to sing; the Flower Woman accepts condolences for her "son" Joe with a wonderfully hypocritical speech; the three artists quarrel; and another guest, the aristocratic Lady Trimmer, unexpectedly quotes Yeats' *Cathleen*. The mourners have become an audience, and they are joined by the Voices who furnish a choral comment on the six dancers, each of whom represents a well-known figure in Irish politics or the arts. Each speaks a brief quotation from the work of one of six men.

In order, the six are W. B. Yeats reciting from his poem "Into the Twilight"; James Joyce slightly misquoting some lines from *Ulysses;* Jonathan Swift composing what seems to be a brief note to Rebecca Dingley, the companion (as Johnston has it later) of the girl the Dean wanted to but could not marry; Oscar Wilde reading a brief excerpt from "De Profundis"; James Mangan repeating some lines from his poem "Dark Rosaleen," already quoted in the melodramatic prologue to the play; and, last, George Bernard Shaw quoting from *John Bull's Other Island.* Why these six? Johnston has said simply that they are "Dublin's greatest contributors to the world's knowledge of itself."[46] Each shadow is received by the stage audience in a different manner, which is presumably a barometer of each man's popularity. The point of each of the six quotations is of a rather general nature; for example, Yeats' lines are addressed to an "Outworn heart in a time outworn" and meant to inspire optimism for a better future for Ireland; Shaw's line comes from the end of his play and refers to the future of an Ireland threatened by take-over by British business interests.

X   *Coda*

After the six, the "shadow" of Emmet, the Speaker, is called forth to "Justify! Justify!" and in this coda for the play we learn the choice that he will make in the dilemma posed by the Blind Fiddler. It should not, of course, be supposed that Emmet has suddenly been elevated to the ranks of the six shadows of the great. On the contrary, he is simply called on to "justify" himself, something he obviously does not do despite the chorus of Voices urging him on with an "Amen" response. In fact, the chorus simply reinforces the point that it is exactly this kind of hero who is assured of welcome and popular approval. (Presumably these Voices are those of the Forms that emerge from the darkness in the first scene of the play set in modern Dublin; the list of Irish names from Burke to Quirke indicates they might be taken as a cross-section of Irish society.)

In language that evokes the Bible, Dante, and Rabelais, the Speaker denounces and repudiates contemporary Ireland which has alternately accepted and rejected him without understanding why it did either. His denunciation includes a part of Emmet's historic Dock Speech, climaxing with two apocalyptic lines from the New Testament (Luke 3:9,17). In a litany of curses, it becomes clear that his condemnation does not spring from any degree of enlightenment but is merely a reaffirmation of his own dream and a rejection of any possible challenge to the dead past. He opts for destruction, the wisdom of fools, a blindness to history, revenge, and a plowshare that can be beaten into a sword. The vision of himself as the creator of a new Ireland which will be a New World pours from his lips as he speaks with godlike authority and messianic fervor:

> I will take this earth in both my hands and batter it into the semblance of my heart's desire![47]
>
> .   .   .   .
>
> I know this garden well for I have called it into being with the Credo of the Invincibles: I believe in the might of Creation, the majesty of the Will, the resurrection of the Word, and Birth Everlasting. (83)

The image of the garden in these lines suggests not only Eden but also the garden of the Priory at Rathfarnham, the home of Sarah and the setting for the old melodrama. As "The Shan Van Vocht" is heard again in the distance, the Speaker's words recall Christ mourning Jerusalem. All memories of Cathleen Ni Houlihann as a raspy-voiced crone, a vampire feeding on her dead sons, are forgotten, and she is now the Old Mother who "will walk the streets of Paradise / Head high, and unashamed." His last lines ("There now. Let my epitaph be written.") are an innocent if ironic parody of the conclusion of Emmet's Dock Speech:

> Let no man write my epitaph: for as no man who knows my motives dare now vindicate them, let not prejudice or ignorance asperse them. Let them and me repose in obscurity and peace, and my tomb remain uninscribed, until other times, and other men, can do justice to my character; when my country takes her place among the nations of the earth, then, and not till then, let my epitaph be written. I have done.

The Ireland that has been revealed in *The Old Lady* does not yet seem ready to "take her place among the nations." The writing of any epitaph for Emmet is premature, and it is the spirit of such unfortunate patriotism — and the romantic adulation of that spirit — that, Johnston implies, would still leave uninscribed any monument to Emmet.

The play, like O'Neill's *The Emperor Jones,* brings the Speaker full circle: through the nightmare that is Dublin, back to the place where he began, the stage of the theater. Robert Emmet had a dream of what a free Ireland could be. He returns, like Shaw's St. Joan in the Epilogue of that play, to see how that dream has reached fruition. Modern Dublin is not a place he knows or likes, nor is it a place where he is known or remembered except vaguely in "story-book" history. To the Lady Trimmers of Dublin drawing rooms, he is "the gentleman who is far from the land," more of the world of "playing" than the real world, and who may, on request, "act something for us" or tell about "wonderful experiences in the Trouble."

The most significant example of contrast in the play is the confrontation of Emmet's vision of Ireland with the reality that independence had finally brought in the half-dozen years since the birth of the Irish Free State. Behind the contrast of the dream and reality is the major purpose of the play: "the exposure of the obstinate vestiges of Emmetism that paralyze the nationhood . . . so recently achieved."[48] Johnston is offering no political panacea, nor is the play making a direct plea for pacifism. But in awareness there is hope. Saddest of all at this time are the "vestiges of Emmetism" that fifty years after independence still provoke violence in both the North and South of Ireland. For example, in June, 1974, the death in an English prison through hunger strike of a confessed robber with some remote I.R.A. connection produced demonstrations in both London and at the funeral in Eire. The troubles are still on Cathleen Ni Houlihan, and she will be talking to her friends.

As a first play, *The Old Lady Says "No!"* is a formidable achievement. Highly theatrical, richly allusive, complex in structure, and still surprisingly relevant in its political implications in addition to being thoroughly entertaining, it is a genuine example of that overworked cliché: a neglected masterpiece of the modern theater.

CHAPTER 2

An Irish Chekhov:
The Moon in the Yellow River

I *From the Gate to the Abbey*

IT is not easy to go better than your first play, if that first play
happens to be *The Old Lady Says "No!"* wrote Thomas
Hogan,[1] and Johnston himself recognized this, for recently he commented that "after you've done an eccentric play like my first...,
you have to write one that's quite straightforward as far as the
presentation is concerned."[2] *The Moon in the Yellow River* is
indeed orthodox, realistic, and straightforward. To some, it was
reminiscent of the great Russian drama with its "almost Chekovian
sense of mood-change rare in Irish dramatists."[3] There is in the
play, wrote Hilton Edwards, a "suggestion of a great undertone
never sounded, a ground bass never actually heard, but whose presence is inevitably implied by the apparently trivial overtones." It is,
he concludes, "the Irish *Cherry Orchard*."[4] *The Moon* might also
be called a history play, and it has rightly been labeled both a problem play and a sequel to *The Old Lady.* Johnston himself termed it
"an exercise in character drawing" and accepted good-naturedly a
curious verdict from England that described it as "a wild Irish farce
by Ireland's latest humorist."[5]

It might seem strange after the definitive approach Edwards and
MacLiammoir had brought to *The Old Lady* — and after the
Abbey's rejection of that play in at least two versions — that Johnston's second play would not automatically become a Gate Theatre
property. But the Gate looked toward broad horizons, encompass-
ing the foreign and experimental. It had, in fact, originated out of a
need to produce in Ireland a kind of play that the Abbey Theatre

42

neither could nor would present. *The Moon,* however, with its conventional plot involving some familiar Irish stage types and containing a necessary theatricality, fitted very well into the repertory of the Abbey, despite the dramatist's critical view of Irish matters of very recent memory. It was the first of four Johnston plays to have its Irish premiere there, and it has been his most successful work for the stage outside Ireland. Apart from English and American productions, it has been given in seven different translations.[6]

II *The Historical Milieu*

In his preface to *The Dreaming Dust* in the collected plays, Johnston wrote that, excepting only *The Moon in the Yellow River,* "all my plays included in the present collection are in various ways historical. That is to say, their very divergent plots have each got a factual basis."[7] It is not necessary, especially when one is considering Johnston's work some forty years later, to exclude his second play as nonhistorical. Even in 1931, it must have been quite apparent to Irish audiences, if not to others, that Johnston was referring, with major alterations it is true, to certain events in Ireland's recent past. The play's historical nuclei, as it were, may be found in two separate events that took place during the early years of the newly formed Irish Free State: the political and military clashes between the new government and the Republicans, and the realization of the Shannon Scheme.

The Anglo-Irish War, which had its most dramatic episode in the Easter, 1916 Uprising in Dublin, came to an end in an agreement signed December 6, 1921, which gave Ireland dominion status in the British Empire. Since the new Irish Free State was to include only twenty-six of the thirty-two counties, the Republicans, who were holding out for complete separation, objected violently to the agreement. Eamon DeValera, the first president elected by the *dail eireann* (Assembly of Ireland), repudiated the agreement, but it was passed over his objections. When he subsequently resigned, a provisional government was set up headed by Michael Collins, a hero of the years of the Troubles. DeValera and the leaders of the Sinn Fein (Ourselves Alone) party refused to participate in its establishment; DeValera went so far as to announce publicly that the provisional government had no authority. Violence erupted in northern Ireland, the area of the six counties excluded from the Irish Free State, and Collins finally agreed to hold a second election which gave a majority to the provisional government and those in favor of the treaty. Still the Republicans did not accept their defeat, and it was at this point that the Irish Republican Army (I.R.A.) began to take the law into its own hands. National anarchy seemed imminent unless drastic measures were taken, and Collins decided to head the army himself.

At the end of 1922, the new Free State faced two important political decisions: the election of a new president (Collins had died in an ambush) and the drafting of a constitution. W. T. Cosgrave was elected to head the government by the new *dail,* and the constitution was framed and ratified on schedule. However, the violence sparked by the I.R.A. continued, and the new government resorted to military force. Court-martials became common, with drastic punishments meted out for minor offenses. In December of 1922, the government, in reprisal for the killing of a member of the *dail,* shot four prisoners (one from each province) without trial. These executions intensified the bitterness of the Republicans, but they did curtail the organized resistance of the I.R.A. At one time, the government held in custody more than twelve thousand prisoners, and there was a total of seventy-seven executions.[8] In the spring of 1923, DeValera called for a cessation of the rebel activities, and the government was finally able to turn to the business of the new state.

What Johnston took from the troubled and complicated history of these years is not very specific. In general, he drew upon three areas: (1) the guerrilla activities of the I.R.A. in their attempts to sabotage the Free State; (2) the reaction of a legal government which, to remain in power, resorted to murder because no other solution to the country's dilemma seemed possible; and (3) the tensions arising out of the construction of a large hydroelectric plant near Limerick.

In Johnston's dramatized account of the troubled months following the treaty with England in January, 1922, an electric power plant modeled on the main station built by the famous Shannon Scheme became the target of the insurgent Republican forces as historically was never the case. Called "the most constructive venture" as well as "one of the biggest political controversies" of the 1920s,[9] the Shannon Scheme was early evidence of the young Free State's ambition not only to bolster the economy with cheap electrical power for industrial and domestic use, but also to distract the attention of the country from the civil disorders of the past years. It was considered wildly impracticable by some who felt Ireland could never use that much electricity. It was also denounced because it was being directed by Germans. In addition, there were objections to industry coming into a society that had for centuries been oriented toward the handmade and the cottage-produced. Ecological objections that the landscape would be ruined and the balance of nature upset were raised as well as objections on theological grounds. Finally, there was the matter of the cost, a fantastic figure for something considered so much of a luxury as electric power.

All of these problems were eventually overcome by the sponsors of the Scheme which was finally to cost, when completed, less than eight million pounds and which took four years to implement.[10] For purposes of his own, Johnston moved the main power station from Limerick to a site near the mouth of the Liffey River and adjacent to the scene of the action of *The Moon*. In making the power plant the objective of a Republican raid, he was able to draw on the tensions the Scheme provoked and blend them with the executions of the insurgents in the early Twenties, creating an atmosphere that is historic even though the characters are not.

III   *Story and Theme*

On a purely narrative level, the plot of *The Moon in the Yellow River* is, except for two incidents, most commonplace and reminiscent of the banal material Chekhov turned into pure gold in his late plays. Tausch, a German engineer in charge of a power station near the coast of Ireland, arrives to visit Dobelle, a distinguished engineer, now retired, who lives nearby with his young daughter. The invitation has been forgotten by the host, and the German is received casually and cautiously by a household composed of Dobelle's eccentric sister, his young daughter, Blanaid, with whom he is not on close terms, his housekeeper, Agnes, and two comic sea-dog friends, George and Potts. Conversation is interrupted by two I.R.A. gunmen who announce that they have come to blow up the power station; yet, one of the gunmen, the son of the housekeeper, assists the German in making a telephone plea to the local authorities for protection. Darrell Blake, the leader of the rebels, has planned the attack so the station will go up just as help arrives. The explosion is to be set off by a shell from a large gun constructed by the two old seamen.

In a mock trial in Act II conducted by Blake, the German is condemned for his interfering efforts to modernize Ireland, but before his impromptu arraignment is quite concluded, Commandant Lanigan arrives with government troops, the gun misfires in the crucial moment, and quite unexpectedly Lanigan kills Blake, his former comrade-in-arms against the English. As Act III begins, Tausch is insisting Lanigan be arrested for the killing, but Dobelle, understanding the necessity of the deed, although not condoning it, refuses to assist him and points out that Tausch and Lanigan are, in fact, on the same side. The fourth and last shell for the big gun is discarded in disgust by the two old cronies, but this is ironically the one that works when it accidentally detonates and destroys the power station. At the end of the play, Dobelle is about to resume the role of father to the daughter he had neglected. Of course, this synopsis, as with any complex work, suggests only superficially the thematic possibilities and the subtleties of construction.

"The theme is international industrialism," wrote Johnston of *The Moon* in his introduction in the collected plays.[11] This is much too narrow a view of the work, and the suggestion that it is a sequel to *The Old Lady* is a proper reminder that the two plays are alike in that "they are based on Ireland's final renunciation of those idealists who would sacrifice life for her, whether the zealots are engaged in struggle against Major Sirr, the symbol of British tyranny, or against Herr Tausch, the symbol of modern machinery."[12] For Constantine Curran, *The Moon* is about neither the Shannon Scheme nor the idealistic conflict of the I.R.A. with the Free State. Rather, the crux of the play is "the interlocking of these themes with the neurosis of Dobelle and the resolution of his bleak nihilism into a renewed harmony with life."[13] Putting it all in rather abstract terms, Robert Hogan rightly singles out Dobelle's speech near the beginning of Act III dealing with the paradox that what is right so often destroys, while what is wrong makes life worthwhile. Johnston's devil's disciple therefore opts for wrong and evil, pain and misery because it is the courageous confrontation with these forces that "makes man so much greater than the angels." But the play's final comment is not one of "bleak nihilism," for Dobelle turns to his young daughter with new understanding and so "affirms the need for human sympathy even in a coldly malevolent world."[14]

IV   Act I: A "Deuced unmannerly house"

The setting of Acts I and III is subtly suggestive of Shaw's *Heart-*

break House. Formerly the officers' barracks in an old fort which overlooks the mouth of a river, this "relic of the Napoleon scare" has been converted into a modern residence, untidy and still furnished with some reminders of its martial past: rusty chains and bolts and iron window shutters beyond which a cannon port may be seen across a courtyard. There is also a cupboard of old blueprints and a large table extending offstage that supports a toy railway system. This is the House of Eire: disordered by its civil embroilments, cluttered with mementos of past battles and outdated blueprints for the future, preoccupied with trivia that are mere tokens of more important things that await fulfillment. The distant hum of turbines from the power station is a constant reminder of the advent of the industrial age encroaching upon and contrasting with the rusty clutter of decades. A ship's siren conveys something of the locale and signals an era of industrialism based on electrical power.

Each act is structured around a series of encounters which, in addition to promoting the plot, are designed to establish and set in opposition assorted points of view. Most of these encounters are well motivated, although the pair of comics often seems to wander in at will. Tausch is usually introduced to a peculiarly Gaelic attitude quite different from his own, although he does not always realize this at first. The opening scene between the German and Agnes constitutes the initial confrontation, for she both opens and closes the play. She is a large boned, red-faced, lower-class version of Mother Ireland, ample of breast and almost overwhelming in her matriarchy. As a minor variant of Cathleen Ni Houlihan, she stands in direct and realistic contrast not only to Yeat's romantic versions but to Johnston's own miserable crone in *The Old Lady*. She is an Ireland commonsensically, if somewhat too narrowly, concerned with the sons and daughters of the future, for throughout the play Agnes considers only the needs of one Mrs. Mulpeter who is about to give birth. Tausch's knocking at the door is ignored through her opening monologue. For her, his "clattering and thumping" are just an extension of "them mechanicalisms" in the powerhouse.

Tausch is an unwelcome intruder in a realm of peace and quiet, for he represents the masculine world of affairs impinging upon the female's domain which nothing symbolizes better than childbirth. More important, he is the symbol of modern machinery — industrialism. He is also an outsider, specifically a German, and therefore from a people devoted to efficiency and technological progress. And like the young girl in Ibsen's *The Master Builder,* he is the future knocking on the door of a reluctant Ireland. In this brief scene where little happens, the slow, unvarying rhythm of the typewriter foreshadows the monotony of a machine-dominated society.

The second encounter, between Tausch and young Blanaid, is confined chiefly to characterizing the girl and her relationship with her father. She is an orphan "unless you count Father," for they do not get on. She longs for convent schooling which will educate her in, among other things, math instead of history and Latin in which she is casually tutored by her aunt. But education will poison the mind, her father says, and so she supposes his mind must be poisoned too — as indeed it is. She has only one friend — Darrell Blake — whom Tausch will meet all too soon, and even he may have dropped her because "We're not awfully good, ... socially, I mean."

George and Potts are Mutt-and-Jeff vaudeville types posing as nautical tosspots, in addition to being the type of comics in which the Abbey now specialized. Only just kept under control, they are comic relief as they go their way expressing grief in humorous fashion, mispronouncing names, and singing risque sea chanties. If their scene has a point, it is merely to introduce the topic of the "big gun" that took four years to construct. One wonders if there was any irony left by 1931 in George's question to the German engineer: "Are you at all interested in guns?"

The most important point of Act I is the encounter between Tausch and Dobelle. It defines two of the four important viewpoints of the play. Dobelle, "a distinguished railway engineer," has the refined sensitivity of an artist tempered with a hint of cruelty that has caused him, Prospero-like, to withdraw from the world, his profession, and even his daughter, to bury himself in his library and amuse himself with a miniature railway. He is satisfied to live in a "Deuced unmannerly house" which hasn't "much to offer" its guests. His retirement is a renunciation of the world, for "I have found that the world you speak of maddens me." For Dobelle, the River Shannon has become "the waters of Lethe," the river of forgetfulness. The reasons for his personal cynicism are not clear until later in the play, although here he has some fairly explicit political comments that describe with detachment the critical situation in Ireland in the early Twenties and could account to some degree for his attitude: "In most countries the political idealist is merely a bore, but here he has a disconcerting tradition of action. He usually has his own Government and his own army as well...."[15] As for Tausch and his project, Dobelle has only warnings: he should not have come to Ireland, and he will find himself out if he stays. It would be much better to leave the powerhouse and go. Dobelle knows the warning will fall on deaf ears.

Inspired in part by Dobelle's work, Tausch is an earnest, intelligent hydroelectrical engineer who eventually, in the midst of Teutonic domestic bliss, answers "the call of romance." When Dobelle responds that it all "sounds like nonsense to me," Tausch is not the least put off. He is sentimental about the family circle he has left and "the charm of the West" he has discovered, while remaining completely naive in regard to Ireland and its people. He is gallant to the unresponsive Aunt Columba, Dobelle's sister, easily put down by Agnes, and much impressed by the industry of George and Potts who have devoted four years to making a big gun plus a year each for four shells. Tausch has come to Ireland out of love and commitment to a talent he thinks is needed and welcomed there. His dedication has brought him to the point of caricaturing German efficiency: "Just a little organization here and you will see the change." As Blake, his nemesis, drives up near the end of Act I, Tausch launches into an aria to electrical power: "I see in my mind's eye this land of the future — transformed and redeemed by power — from the sordid trivialities of peasant life to something newer and better. Soon you will be a happy nation of free men — free not only by the magic of empty formulae or by the colour of the coats you wear, but by the inspiration of power — power — power" (34).

This hymn to electricity is cut short by a farcical scene in which Willie Reilly demonstrates the I.R.A.'s inefficiency (as compared with the German) when he engages his mother, Agnes, in a quick skirmish and is demolished by her. Willie is governed by orders when he is not governed by his mother; it is his single-mindedness and somewhat simple devotion that potentially shape him into Lanigan's killer at some future time. Now, however, his idea is to blow up the power station, but with typical Irish efficiency, the explosives are damp and won't touch off. This is only one of a series of mishaps that occur throughout the play and dominate much of the action.

Darrell Blake is depicted as a "man of action," who can view his own violent deeds rather whimsically. Why he wants to blow up the power station is not resolved very satisfactorily. Blake suggests only that it is to be done in the name of revolution: "A beautiful word." This is perhaps enough to indicate that he is a version of the idealistic young rebel, like Emmet, who sees the goals of the future, inasmuch as he sees them at all, as attainable only through force. Act I concludes on a madly comic note as Willie tries to put through the German's call to the local fire brigade to come and save the station he himself is preparing to blow up. Except for the humor in the scene, one could sympathize with Tausch's assessment: "I think I go mad!"

Aunt Columba gets her name from a sixth-century Irish saint who was a famous pupil of the noted monastery school at Clonard where Latin was held in high esteem; hence her insistence that Blanaid study it. She is another aspect of Ireland, a little mad in her own special devotion to causes, extremely suspicious of strangers, and smugly mysterious in her warning that the power station is in danger. It is a little difficult to be sure of the basis of Aunt Columba's objections to Tausch and the station; presumably they are partly political and partly ecological, although her righteous indignation at mankind's presumption in harnessing a force of nature cannot be ignored.

V   Act II: An Ecological Melodrama

The setting for Act II is a storeroom for the Coast Life Saving Service (thus accounting for the presence of George and Potts who belong to that branch) which, while obviously different from the Dobelle living room, is similarly evocative and symbolic. This one-time post of the Army Ordnance Corps retains reminders of both its martial past and English presence in the protruding muzzle of the big gun and the four projectiles, the barred window, and the Royal Arms over the fireplace. But unlike the living room, which represents the present to the family, this room is their dumping place, their attic where they store away the past. In addition to trunks and furniture, there is also a piano, a reminder of Dobelle's sensitivity which he suppresses, and some portraits stored in sacking. One of these is of Dobelle's wife who died in Germany giving birth to Blanaid. Finally, to emphasize that the room is another view of Ireland, there are government circulars relating to distress signals and fog horns for sounding warnings, in addition to the life-saving rockets. In charge of things, significantly, are the two incurable romantics, George and Potts, who deal in handmade guns and ships constructed in bottles, a neat parallel with Dobelle's toy railroad. In short, the setting is a symbolic portrait of an Ireland in distress controlled by inefficient, would-be lifesavers who think small, build slowly, and act effectively only by accident.

Act II is organized with more variety but still reflects Johnston's technique of contrast. There are three encounters that amount to serious confrontations. The first moments are pleasantly time-filling, designed to establish a six-minute overlap with Act I. Aunt Columba is heard again offstage repeating the last part of her prediction of disaster with all the fervor of an Old Testament prophet, and Willie's intrusion on Tausch while he is trying to telephone for help is clearly seen as no accident. He has, in fact, been sent by Blake, his commander, who is enjoying the foreigner's discomfiture, to assist the German. Blake's plan has the ingenuity of a comic strip: he will allow, even help, Tausch to call for protection, but he will see to it that such assistance will arrive too late. He only regrets being unable to enjoy the German's anger at the destruction.

The scene shifts gears by focusing on Dobelle who discovers in the effects stacked about the room the old portrait of his wife, "something I've been looking for for months." This portrait is, as Johnston put it, "a gift of the past to the present,"[16] a reminder of the love that was and a foreshadowing of its rebirth at the end of the play in the father's newly discovered need for his daughter. The emptiness of their present relationship is characterized in Blanaid's overture of friendship to her father by offering him a diary Blake has given her, a gift he rejects. In contrast to this pathetic encounter, there is the farce of the awkward Willie who drops one of the four shells for the gun which fails to explode. These four shells, like the four gospels to Blake, facetiously suggest his dedication to the violence they presage. "So much for Matthew," he says of the first dud in this comic moment of Irish inefficiency.

In the first of the four important encounters in this act, Blake reveals to Tausch the motive for the rebellious and destructive act he is planning. Political alignments do not loom that large in his reasoning; what seems to dominate Blake's thinking is his romantic antipathy to the machine as a harbinger of technological progress that deadens man's capacity for enjoying life while freeing him so that he could do just that. His reasoning is idealistic and retrogressive to the point of being slightly quaint, even for the late 1920s.

"Listen to the noise of your turbines and then come back and give me any adequate reason for it all," Blake tells Tausch. "The rest of the world may be crazy, but there's one corner of it yet, thank God, where you and your ludicrous machinery haven't turned us all into a race of pimps and beggars" (52). To Tausch's altogether reasonable reply that the result needn't be "pimps and beggars" but might, in fact, be advancement for "backward countries," Blake replies that technology is "just another shackle on your limbs," and one that is self-inflicted at that. "I might be like you, Herr Tausch, if I chose, and this country might be like yours if you had your way. But I don't choose, and you won't have your way. Because we intend to keep one small corner of the globe safe for the unfortunate human race" (53). All very well, but such high-flown sentiments coming from a rebel who admittedly does not know "the dangerous end" of a gun bespeaks a woeful ignorance of the everyday problems of the country in which he lives.

At this point, the second of the four shells (Mark) for the "muzzle-loading, four-inch-slow-firing-Potts-shot" fails, and there follows from Potts a humorous story of his wife's death. In an effort to save her when their ship seemed to be sinking, he and George put the lady into the only life belt and threw her overboard, only to find her later floating upside down when they realized that the boat was merely aground in shallow water, and all was well. This little parable of throwing out the baby with the bath water is a perfect comic parallel to the inane attempt to destroy the power station.

The brief scene between Dobelle and Aunt Columba sharply draws the battle lines over Blanaid as well as dramatizing the father's unwillingness to function in his role as parent. "I deny all duties and privileges where Blanaid is concerned," he maintains. "I will feed and clothe her, but there my interests end" (57). It is clear that his sour view of Ireland, the world in general, and his family in particular owes much to his wife's death at his daughter's birth. Furthermore, her education, particularly in regard to sex, is being retarded at his insistence; since he distrusts education, he resorts to the "ignorance is bliss" cliché, especially when the bliss is sexual.

The argument between Blake and Tausch is revived again in a scene that leads into the climactic shooting. To Blake's ultimatum that Tausch may do what he likes with his own world, but "I insist that you leave me mine," the German replies that "This world is neither yours nor mine. It belongs to all these people. Have you the right to say that I may not help them?'' (58). But is his help wanted, Blake asks, and what follows is one of those "trial scenes" that in plays of ideas function dialectically to provide a hearing for several viewpoints and climax in a judgment *à la The Madwoman of Chaillot.*

As they await the arrival of the authorities on the scene, Blake arraigns the German on the charge that he is interfering in Ireland's affairs. Johnston the barrister is in the foreground as Blake begins the trial by charging that Tausch "has outraged the sacred person of our beloved mother — Cathleen ni Houlihan'' and thus he should be condemned and his work — the station — destroyed (59). The witnesses are polled, and some of their reactions are highly humorous. After trying to avoid the issue by saying he is on duty, Willie decides that the station may be blown up because rebuilding it would create employment. George and Potts object because firing the big gun would destroy the shells they took so long to make. Aunt Columba's objections are forcefully registered and seem to center on man's becoming dependent on the machine and therefore on the men who control it. Agnes objects to the noise for the same reasons as before: "The whirring thrum of them mechanicalisms is very distrubing to poor Mrs. Mulpeter.''

The trial takes on its greatest significance when Dobelle seizes the chance to speak his true sentiments (which will be elaborated on later in the play's most important speech). To him, Tausch is "a servant of righteousness," and he has sworn allegiance to the other side. "You wish to serve something you call progress," he tells the German. "But progress — whatever it is — is never achieved by people like you who pursue it. Progress is the fruit of evil men, with sinister motives. You and your kind can only make misery'' (65). Herein lies the play's paradox that so torments Dobelle and is the crux of his nihilism: evil men and evil deeds seem to bring about progress, while righteousness seems to have the opposite effect. In an ironic inversion worthy of Shaw, Dobelle sounds here like the devil's disciple.[17]

In the play's climactic scene, the big gun misfires, the Republican raid fails, and Commandant Lanigan must deal with the captured saboteurs. Particularly sad is the situation in which patriots who once fought together for their country now find themselves on opposite sides in a civil brawl and resort to killing their former comrades. Both Blake and Lanigan had evidently been active in the struggle with England, but Lanigan sided with those who found the

Free State an acceptable compromise, while Blake belonged to the group that held out for complete separation from England and an independent Irish republic for the whole island. Blake is an insouciant idealist who seems as concerned with the natural landscape as he is with political terrain; Lanigan is a pragmatic realist who will do whatever is necessary to keep the government (to which there is no viable alternative) alive and functioning.

As Willie raves that Tausch has called in the Staters to use force in saving the power station ("Might against right. That's not playing the game, you know"), Blake denounces Lanigan as a polluter of the earth. Tausch, in his turn, bitterly inveighs against being the butt of the joke, the victim of their talk. "...I am the only one who will ever *do* anything in this place," he charges. Ireland is a "damned debating society"; everybody talks but "nothing ever happens" (69–70). In counterpoint to Tausch's angry remonstrances is the lovely song Blake sings here to his own accompaniment. It is Ezra Pound's translation of a Chinese poem ("Fu-I loved the green hills"), and it provides, of course, the title for the play:

> Fu-I loved the green hills
> And the white clouds.
> Alas he died of drink.
>
> And Li-Po
> Also died drunk.
> He tried to embrace a Moon
> In the Yellow River.

Blake, the romantic dreamer and the rebel intoxicated by misguided patriotism, loved the green hills and white clouds of Ireland. But in trying to realize his pastoral dream of an independent island unpolluted by man or machine, he died, like Li-Po, trying to embrace a beatiful ideal.

On Tausch's last line that "nothing ever happens" but talk, Lanigan shoots Blake, "without any demonstration," as if to disprove the German's remark. This is a marvelously dramatic curtain for Act II, reminiscent of Chekhov's final curtain in *The Sea Gull*. Johnston has noted that sometimes there is no applause at all at the end of this act, which "oddly enough, ... is regarded by those who know the play well, not as a disgrace, but as an indication of a really fine performance."[18]

VI Act III: Resolution and Renewal

The opening minutes of Act III, a brief anthology of the eccentric, the ridiculous, and the paradoxical, soon culminate in an important dialogue between brother and sister, containing possibly the most important speech in the play. The old matter of Blanaid's need for companionship and a systematic exposure to a traditional education leads to the aunt's reminder that although her brother is against religion, he should remember that "they only did what was right by Mary [Dobelle's wife] and the child according to their lights." This, of course, is just the problem, that although it was the "right" thing to sacrifice the mother's life for the child's, yet doing "right" deprived him of her. The paradox that right and wrong seem to bring about exactly the opposite results is the soul-sickness that has caused Dobelle to withdraw into himself and into a miniature world characterized by the toy train, a world not big enough for either his daughter, whom he ignores, or his sister, with whom he seems only to argue. He is not against religion, only "rightness," he insists. "It is always evil that seems to have made life worth while, and always righteousness that has blasted it. And now I solemnly say that I believe in wrong. I believe in evil and in pain and decay and, above all, in the misery that makes man so much greater than the angels" (74). Although the "right causes pain" theme derives from Dobelle's own personal situation, it has other wider applications throughout the play, one of which is obviously the political dilemma of those forced to kill out of necessity and sustain a government through murder.

Now that Tausch has provoked the situation that resulted in Blake's death, he is in a moral bind and wants to disclaim any responsibility for it by blaming Lanigan. It is simple murder, he insists. Replies Lanigan, "Why not call it war?" But moments later he agrees with the German: "I was a rebel once. What I've done was war then. Now I'm on the other side and it's murder" (78). Tough and realistic in a way the others are not, he knows himself for what he is. He realizes that he is perpetuating the national legacy of political assassination in an attempt to safeguard civil order, that he is destroying its citizens to save the country. Without being particularly clever or intelligent, he is in his own eyes simply doing what he considers necessary. However, he retreats into familiar excuses for political violence: someone has to do the country's killing; he's only doing his job; the country needs deeds not words.

Furthermore, he knows that even as he has killed Blake, he will himself almost certainly be killed.

Trying to counter Tausch's Teutonic regard for the forms of justice, Lanigan explains that Blake would have wanted a swift and immediate execution, not "a lot of play-acting in court" followed by a long jail term. He also recognizes the importance of his role as state executioner, the necessity of it, as he thinks: "I'm a gunman. I always was and I always will be.... But God help you all if I wasn't. It may be brains and inspiration that makes the country at the start, but it's my help you're always telephoning for before the end" (80). Any residue of passion over the killing of Blake will become a matter of personal vengeance, says Lanigan, "between me and the likes of Willie Reilly." And so it goes on, one death after another in the frightening tradition of Irish political life, a process Lanigan recognizes without being able to terminate.

Tausch, however, is only able to see that the rules are broken. He will finally be defeated by his experience in a foreign land, while Dobelle, because he has lived within the paradox that evil spawns right, recognizes and ultimately profits from the lesson Lanigan effectively teaches that there is more than one way in which a man may die for his country.

A coda follows this vital scene. Refusing to share responsibility for the killing, Tausch hesitates to denounce Lanigan for murder; he prefers to think he and Blake might have reached a truce after which they could live in a state of mutual respect without agreeing with each other. After all, they are both romantic types, each longing for a different world, each willing to make some sacrifice to create it. But although he does not like Lanigan, Dobelle will take no part in denouncing him, and he tries to explain to the German how his world is antithetically opposed to Blake's. "You'd always have been disturbing the waters with your machinery and drowning his moon in mud," and "in the end you would either have had to kill him or to give up your fight" (82). There follows the only moment in the play when Tausch is on the verge of recognizing the central paradox: "I wonder why the people whom we can like most easily are always on the wrong side?" The shot that killed Blake was, figuratively speaking, triggered by Tausch who barely understands what Dobelle has been trying to tell him: that Lanigan's shot was part of his world and that he and Lanigan are really on the same side. More than that, Dobelle continues, "Lanigan is just yourself. He is your finger on the trigger. Denounce him by all

means. . . . But before you denounce him, I say you must give me
an answer to what he has said. And you won't do that. Because
there is no answer, and you know it'' (82). True, there is no answer
to the cycle of killings, and that is the tragedy of both the real and
the dramatic situations. But there is one fact: the power station
remains.

Only, of course, it doesn't — not for long. In one of those incon-
spicuous, seemingly pointless, and slightly comic moments of the
play, Aunt Columba has rescued the fourth shell (this one would be
named for St. John) for the now-confiscated gun by bringing it into
the living room under a tea-cosy. George and Potts, sick of the
whole episode, decide to chuck it over the wall on to an old slag
heap. As the turbines hum and dawn begins to break, Tausch ser-
monizes to Dobelle about the purpose of life that transcends individual problems. "Everything you see has its purpose in the scheme
of things," he says, the river, the pier, the turbine house, "Everything with a purpose." Inquires Dobelle: "Even the slag heap?" At
that moment the fourth shell finally honors its builders. In a flash
and a roar, the power station is destroyed — by chance, by
accident.

In a final summation after the catastrophe, Dobelle rhetorically
addresses Tausch who has just departed: "You'll never learn anything, and I'll never do anything," he says. "There's no end and
there's no solution" (86). The German will not be discouraged; he
will build again someplace, and he will not "go mad." The moral
dilemma that has emotionally incapacitated Dobelle will remain,
but there also remains the possibility of love, not as a way out, of
course, but as the best alternative available. The conclusion is a
serious parody of Mrs. Tancred's prayer (and later, Juno's lament)
from O'Casey's *Juno and the Paycock:* O'Casey's lines, "take
away our hearts o' stone, and give us hearts o' flesh! Take away this
murdherin' hate, an' give us Thine own eternal love!" become simply "Take away this cursed gift of laughter and give us tears
instead."

The final moments of the play in which father is reconciled with
daughter are open to the charge of sentimentality, but dramatically,
this is a quite acceptable resolution of Dobelle's dilemma on a personal level. Here, at least, there may be some kind of solution, that
"renewed harmony with life," which is all an individual may hope
to salvage from the shipwreck of the state. There will be no moon
in the Yellow River for these characters, but as events are still

proving, Irishmen need to view matters in the light of common day.

Last of all, there is Agnes who endures. In a bit of pantomime that concludes the play, she opens the shutters to let in a new day and hums a lullabye. Mrs. Mulpeter has been delivered of her child, and this raw-boned Cathleen is satisfied and with the promise of new life looks optimistically on the face of the ravaged land. Theatrical and not particularly subtle, it is the most optimistic note in an otherwise somber view of the days ahead for the Irish Free State.

For some, *The Moon in the Yellow River* is a witty and beautiful play; for others, it does not quite succeed in uniting its several elements. It is an entertaining and highly theatrical play that attempts to speak with humor, sophistication, and wisdom through characters that are distinct and significant creations. It is, admittedly, a rather "talky" work but one that ambitiously tackles a host of topics pertaining to Ireland in the Twenties. It is to the play's credit, if not to Ireland's, that it is still relevant, nor is its relevance limited to the Irish.

CHAPTER 3

The Mythic Quest:
A Bride for the Unicorn

I *Problems*

DENIS Johnston's next play, *A Bride for the Unicorn,* appeared in 1933, two years after *The Moon in the Yellow River.* It was obviously not an Abbey play since it was even more experimental than *The Old Lady,* so it naturally went to the Gate Theatre where it opened May 9. In its ambitious attempts to go beyond the experimentation of its predecessor, the *Bride* presented Johnston with the most problems he encountered in writing any of his plays: "Indeed, I doubt if I ever solved some of them. It was a kind of play for which there was no prototype that I was aware of at the time, and it was trying to do something that I still don't believe is possible on the stage — that is to say, to deal with an idea that is not already   consciously or subconsciously — in the mind of the audience" [1].

Bride is both substantial in content and ambitious in technique, but it does not quite work. And the subject is not, as the dramatist suggests, altogether the source of the trouble. First of all, the play is too long; there is much that is dispensable. The dialogue is too often pretentious in style, too determined to employ diverse allusions to bolster myth, too varied in form, ranging as it does from frivolous repartee to portentous pronouncements, from rhymes with the innocence of the nursery to choral comments of a pseudo-Hellenic sort. It is highly complex in its many scenes with diverse settings, its dependence on a multi-level stage, its use of music for

59

purposes of contrast and parody, and its attempts to construct a myth that will be operative, to some extent, on several levels. Johnston had better control of his material in *The Old Lady* where the action, as in Strindberg's *Dream Play,* was governed by a single conciousness and where the range of allusion and myth was not so wide.

Bride is undoubtedly the playwright's most ambitious play though hardly his best one. Over forty years later, it still seems a unique and highly complex work, and there are not many plays with which it may be compared. Una Ellis-Fermor has called it "one of the most original pieces of dramatic technique in the Irish drama."[2] It is not, Johnston insists, an Expressionistic drama, and he does not want it approached that way. It may best be viewed as a rather complicated morality play or an allegory which relies on myth. However, the allegory is rather loose, for in many scenes one is not conscious of it at all, while the myth is present as a mere framework and a series of allusions.

II   *The Story*

The *Bride* opens with a Prelude set in "an aery timeless region." He and She — a gentleman in a dressing gown and a lady — meet several players, called the "Seven Companions," who are to participate in a play. Lines are handed out to the seven by the gentleman who identifies himself simply as the Observer. Nothing further is learned about the lady except that she is not merely in the play; she *is* the play. In scene two, the story of a young man, John, begins at Dr. Paddlewick's Academy where he and the seven, now schoolboys, are getting ready to go home for Christmas holidays. A tippling bust in the schoolroom tempts John with the promise of an introduction to a masked lady who then appears out of the side of a tall clock. The lady (She of the Prelude) almost immediately arouses a youthful passion in John, and as the clock strikes twelve, they move off to the accompaniment of a wedding march for the nuptial night. After a brief interlude, the bridal party arrives around two A.M. in the lobby of a hotel where the seven are having a noisy gathering. Somewhat later, John appears from his room to announce that his bride has vanished. By this time, the clock's hands show four A.M.

The next morning John appears in school, transformed by his brief night of love. Now he is obsessed with the idea that he must search for his lost bride. The seven undertake to raise money to help with the quest. By ten A.M., John, although still haunted by the memory of his bride, decides to settle for Doris, pretty but ordinary. In the last scene in Part I, the seven go energetically, and sometimes dishonestly, about their fund-raising in order to assist John in his search for his first bride.

In the opening scene of Part II, it is clear that John's marriage to Doris has not proved a very happy one; he is only too pleased to use the excuse of meeting one of his seven friends to get away from wife and home and seek consolation in the neighborhood pub where he gets drunk, encounters Time, Doubt, and his Shadow, and finally attacks a clock similar to the one from which appeared the masked lady. For the damage and disturbance he has caused in the pub, John is brought to trial and eventually given a suspended sentence. At this point, he is drafted for wartime military duty. Although he is anxious to engage the enemy, he finds his foe is merely one of his seven school friends. When both refuse to fight, peace is declared, and the scene shifts to the conference table. Here all seven appear again with John; in a great outburst, he mourns his coming death and lost love, asking what he has done to be separated from her. The drunken bust appears with the masked lady who reveals her face to John. He embraces her and then dies, clutching at her cloak which collapses to reveal empty air. There is a brief coda for the two main parts which is essentially a celebration of John's death.

What happens is reasonably clear, but why it happens and what it signifies is not. Nor is the significance of characters or even their identities very clear. It is at this point, whether seeing the play, reading it, or analyzing it, that one realizes the demands it makes. Of course, no synopsis is really adequate, but it will serve as a reminder of what is happening on the most literal level. But what of the theme? And what of the allegoric and mythic levels?

III   *Mythos and Meaning*

It is easy enough to come up with several interpretations of the play, and it is to Johnston's credit that all of them are significant. The playwright has not settled for small targets here. The play is about life, death, love, time, and a quest — individually or collectively. Johnston himself, perhaps in some vexation that a play he liked has posed such difficulties, has stated several times that what the play is about as far as he is concerned is "the proposition that the fear of death is an illusion, and does not really exist at all.'' And this is not just a question of stoicism, he insists. ''What the play tries to say is that everything we do is directed at accomplishing what we regard as our 'maturity' — our fulfillment — which, after all, is only another word for death. So, you see, it's absurd to be afraid that it may come too soon, when the thing that we're afraid of turns out to be the very thing we're seeking.''[3] On another occasion, he put it in a slightly different, if more succinct, way. The *Bride* is ''supposed to be a statement that the business of life is itself, and that its crown is its ending, and that consciously or subconsciously we are aware of this, and that most of our activities show our awareness.''[4]

The play, then, is about the search of John Foss for his own death, the end that will give meaning to his life and the end that, as Johnston has it, is the point toward which his life has been moving. Allegorically, John Foss is Everyman, since the course of life toward death is every man's movement. His first name is one of the most common as well as the English equivalent of Juan, the name of the archetypal lover. His last name, Foss, comes from the first syllable, anglicized, of phosphorus (in the original production he was called John Phosphorus), which again evokes the Everyman condition by suggesting a necessary chemical constituent for life. Phosphorus is also light-producing and symbolically links John with Apollo, the sun god, in some of the choral passages. The masked lady he embraces at the end is Death for whom he has been searching ever since his first encounter with her. The Seven Companions embody seven different types of men, seven different approaches to life, or perhaps seven different qualities which compounded make up the fabric of most men's lives. The Ulitmate Observer is, one on level, some objective Power who foresees the play-script of John's life without the power to write it. The drunken bust — one critic, with a look back to *The Old Lady,* has called him a ''debauched Grattan''[5] — is the Collective Wisdom of Mankind who, in his more relaxed moments and when John turns to him, occasionally offers guidance and a few answers.

On the mythic level, John is Jason searching for the Golden Fleece; the seven friends are seven of Jason's companions who accompanied him on that archetypal quest. Actually, the myth does not seem to add that much here, but it does function, along with other allusions, to give John heroic stature. Finally, the quest for the lost bride is a universal theme. There are other passing references to history and myth throughout — Pandora, King Arthur, Charlemagne, Pericles and Aspasia, Castor and Pollux, Sophia the Great Mother of Gnosticism — which are meant to strengthen and expand to an even greater degree the idea of the heroic quest. Unfortunately, these allusions are too often appendages that complicate the drama without illuminating it to any great extent, quite different from the carefully integrated quotations in *The Old Lady*.

IV   *The Dimensions of Time*

The most difficult aspect of *A Bride for the Unicorn* is the problem of time. Essential to the play's construction is a theory of time known as Serialism which Johnston learned from the English philosopher J. W. Dunne, whose book entitled *An Experiment with Time* (1929) was very popular in the 1930s and is still in print in England. According to Serialism, time is composed of a series of dimensions that stretch infinitely and exist simultaneously. It also posits "the existence of a reasonable kind of 'soul' — an individual soul which has a definite beginning in absolute Time — a soul whose *immortality, being in other dimensions of time, does not clash with the obvious ending of the individual in the physiologist's Time dimension....*"[6] This theory stands in contrast to the conventional linear conception of time as centered in the present but extending into a future and retreating into a past. Dunne's term for this familiar concept is Time One. He submits that since we are, of course, conscious of operating in Time One, it would be paradoxical for us to be both actor and observer at once. So somewhere outside and beyond Time One, there is another dimension which is the vantage point of the observer, that part of the individual who looks on as the other part acts.

It might be well to note at this point that Dunne came to this theory through a study of dreams and the belief that, far from referring only to events of the past, dreams refer as well and as often to events of the future. If this is so, then the dreamer would have all of Time One revealed to him — past, present and future — a total present without beginning or end. The dreamer would then be observing from that next dimension which Dunne calls Time Two.

Time, then, though beyond space, becomes for Dunne just another dimension, the fourth, which is open, like the three-dimensional world, to an observer in Time Two, which then becomes a fifth dimension. Dunne calls this consciousness that observes ordinary time the Ultimate Observer, for to such an observer life is viewable not just as a line but totally and spatially. Moreover, it would be true that at least two dimensions of time are continually operative via the observer in the fifth dimension. It would also follow that in another dimension — the sixth — Time Two would appear as a spatial entity. If there is a consciousness, then, that observes in the fifth dimension (i.e., in Time Two), it logically follows that there is another "observing self" in the sixth dimension who may survey the entire fifth dimension. And so on and on through a whole series of such observers and a literally infinite series of time dimensions. Obviously in this theory there is a consciousness that never dies. In fact, the first observer is the only one who would cease to observe, though the inference is that even he survives the destruction of the brain.

And this is what intrigued Johnston about Dunne's theory: the possibility of an immortality not based on the supernatural or the theological, an immortality that did not require God, faith, or worship. It is a cold mathematical argument which seems to offer the warm consolation of an eternal consciousness, if not eternal life as theologically conceived. The emphasis has shifted from life as preparation to life as fulfillment, from death to be feared to death as ultimate goal. Viewed in the light of Dunne's theory, *A Bride for the Unicorn* may be interpreted as a heroic morality play in which the soul, John, first briefly encounters a vision of the fulfillment of death in a moment of love with the masked lady, Death itself. Life then becomes a quest to reexperience that fulfillment at the same time that it continues on a more mundane plane — in John's case, the marriage with Doris. The reunion with the masked lady at the end is fulfillment as well as death, but only death in Time One. Beyond is a consciousness in another time dimension, and physical death is only a means of moving from one time dimension to another.

V   *The Prelude*

The Prelude is just that, a scene with music prefacing the action. Music is important throughout the play, not only to accompany the action but also to suggest a particular point in time: perhaps some period of John's life in Time One or, as in the Prelude, in Time Two, an "aery timeless region." It is "cold wintry music" that is heard even before the house lights go down. This music of Time Two blends with the music the lady is playing on the piano, suggesting the ultimate harmony of Death with consciousness in Dunne's fifth dimension. The music ends in chords like the chiming of hours which foreshadow the beginning of Time One for the action of scene two. At this point, however, the action is "timeless"; the pendulum above the piano is stationary, and the clock has no hands. Johnston has borrowed from Dunne both the handless clock and, with a change, the lady's sheet music (without time annotations).[7]

Later, when the clock is suddenly endowed with hands and the pendulum is set in motion, Time One is understood to prevail. The lady's piano solo becomes a duet when she is joined by another player behind a curtain who eventually introduces himself as the Ultimate Observer, perhaps Johnston's most obvious borrowing from Dunne. In this Observer, the playwright is dramatizing as a separate character what Dunne sees as simply another aspect of the same person, in this case, John Foss. A flower, first seen on the piano and in evidence somewhere throughout most of the play, symbolizes the beauty and vitality of love, specifically John's love for the masked lady and the attraction of death as the fulfillment for which he has been searching.

Such action as there is in the Prelude centers on assigning "parts" to the seven players who are named, in the tradition of the morality play, after abstract qualities which, in varying proportions, constitute the life of John the Everyman: wisdom (Leonard the Learned), prosperity (Percy the Prosperous), love (Lewis the Loving), courage (Bernard the Brave), greed (Albert the Acquisitive), charity (Harold the Helpful), and most important, eccentricity, that special and particular insight that sets one individual apart from another (Egbert the Eccentric). The "parts" assigned to the seven seem more on the order of roles in a play, but the Ultimate Observer refers to them as musical parts, though as yet without the annotations of time. Egbert, who is more alert than the other six and who sometimes seems to speak for the author, notes the omission and inquires, "What is the time?" (referring to the music) which is one way of putting the key question. The Observer replies that "if we could answer Egbert's question, we could answer all questions. We would be Gods, and there would be no purpose in this play at all. For that is just what it is all about. What is the time?"[8]

These lines direct attention to the fact that the play will function in more than one dimension of time, both from scene to scene and simultaneously within the same scene. Time sequences will, in fact, be scrambled so that it is often difficult to tell exactly at what point in John's life the scenes are occurring. In general, however, they move from youth to age. The Observer is a narrator ("Let me tell you the story") somewhat on the order of a Brechtian storyteller. John, he says, is to be created and endowed "with the mystery of the hours and of the seasons." In "The Delphic Hymn to Apollo" that concludes the Prelude, the hero is presumably being celebrated not only as "Phoebus of the golden hair" but also as Plato's Charioteer who drives the horses of body and soul. The most important of the several references in this first scene, however, is to John as the mythical Jason searching for the Fleece with his Seven Companions who are also compared to Charlemagne's twelve peers, the Paladins.

It might be well to pause and ask how and why Johnston is off to a bad start, for what is wrong with the Prelude is symptomatic of what is wrong with the play. The varied uses of music throughout work most of the time. The Ultimate Observer is effective so far, even if an audience were not aware — and most would not be — that Johnston had borrowed his name and capacities from Dunne. The seven players are engaging with their brisk if not scintillating repartee. What mars the prologue is the preponderance of allusions. For example, why the reference to the Paladins? Is John to be compared with Charlemagne? If so, to what point? "Chained like Prometheus to an icy peak," is John also somehow Promethean? Does all this add to or detract from Johnston's use of the Jason myth to strengthen the quest motif? Is the Observer "playing" a musical composition or narrating a story or doing both in addition to appearing as a participant (the Bust) in the action? Finally, the role of the lady, She, is unfocused here. She is a "supernatural being" outside time with her blank music sheets and handless clock. Seemingly to her surprise, she is to be involved in the "play" but not really *in* it; she *is* it. And again, is "it" story, play, or musical composition or all three? Without wishing to split hairs in regard to this admirably ambitious play, it might be submitted that the structural concept is weak as a result of trying to include too much. It is literary overkill.

VI *Everyman's Progress*

The play proper includes scenes ii through xi, plus a coda which is really a musical finale in the guise of a tribute to the dead hero. These scenes comprise John's life from his schooldays to his death. His story is a *Pilgrim's Progress* of sorts in which the hero achieves a consummation of life only through death. When he is introduced in scene ii, he is a schoolboy at Dr. Paddlewick's Academy for young gentlemen. Immediately the major themes of time, life, and love are sounded. This scene is the first to be set in Time One, but when, in his first speech, he ponders the possibility of "one enigmatic moment — when yesterday, to-morrow and to-day are one," John is clearly, without realizing it, referring to Dunne's Time Two. Nor is he sure what is meant when he is told to "Prepare for Life." For him, life so far is unknown, and so the objectives of life are unknown as well as how to achieve them. John does not know how to speak of love, but he recognizes that the Christmas carols outside are secular choruses from "The Song of Solomon" celebrating love and fertility in the season of spiritual rebirth through Christ.

The motif of the heroic quest is introduced and parodied by a casual order from Leonard the Learned (here a master of the school) to look for his umbrella. The most significant development in this scene from John's schooldays is the appearance of the drunken bust of Lynceus, the navigator for the Argonauts on their journey for the Golden Fleece. He is to be John's guide of sorts. The Bust, of course, is also the He of the Prelude as well as the Ultimate Observer who sees from his vantage point in Time Two the whole course of John's life. His function here is to introduce John to "a very distinguished visitor," and from the side of the clock he produces She, who now wears a mask resembling her real features and carries the flower that had been in the vase on her piano. For John, this is the symbolic emancipation by Time from Death. He is presented to her as "an estimable boy, a primrose of respectability, whose virgin couch is empty and whose heart is whole." In turn, she is presented to John, "her swift limbs whispering desire."

Soon, the group adjourns to a hotel to the strains of a wedding march. To signify the importance of the wedding, the pendulum of the clock begins to swing, and the heretofore handless dial suddenly acquires hands and begins to strike twelve. For John, his life in Time One begins the moment he accepts the masked lady for his bride. He now has the complete cycle of one day, twenty-four hours (a metaphor for a lifetime), to consummate his love, lose his bride and find her again. After the sexual initiation of his bridal night, John reappears, his manner somewhat changed. Johnston employs the initiation into sex as a metaphor for his Everyman's brief glimpse into another world, the world of Time Two with its simultaneous view of past, present, and future. As though in a dream, John has received a fleeting revelation: the proper end of life and its culmination is death toward which men unconsciously desire to move since it is the final fulfillment, the ripeness that is all. This revelation, this momentary glimpse into the heart of light, Johnston locates in the sex act. But as the moment of passion is brief, so is the vision, and he is left with only the memory which motivates and sustains a lifelong quest to find his lost bride and regain, through her, the passion of that revelation.

The quest is on in scene iv, and John Foss/Jason has been joined by his seven aggressive and resourceful companions. However, John, on whose behalf they go adventuring, is not quite the same person they had known. He has seen "beauty, fierce and unashamed" and as a result has become a "very fierce and terrible man."

By scene v, the clock measuring off the cycle of John's life has advanced to ten A.M., the springtime of his life. As he moves further in time from the experience of love with the masked lady, the intensity of his passion for her diminishes, and he is tempted to compromise it by proposing to the fair-haired Doris who is merely "pretty in an obvious kind of way." There is a very interesting blurring of time in this scene, for it is both happening and has already happened. John seems to find the pastoral setting for his proposal to Doris a familiar one, and Egbert, by now something of a surrogate for the Bust, prods him into admitting that there had been "some little foolishness" in his life and that "this might be the same girl," even as he is about to betray his vision and repeat a scene with Doris that he has evidently already played some years before. So while John is operating in Time One, there is in this scene a suggestion of *déjà vu* to account for this curious amalgam of the event and his recollection of it. His wooing of Doris proceeds with a sentimental rhetoric that is nearly matched by her banal responses and concludes with Egbert's singing of "Sumer is icumen in."

John's marriage with Doris the "Spring Goddess" is reviewed in scene vii at two P.M. This is probably one of the most successful scenes in the play, for though it is evidently to be played realistically, it seems to half-glance over its shoulder at the stream-of-consciousness technique of O'Neill's *Strange Interlude,* at the same time foreshadowing the comic methods of a play like Eugène Ionesco's *The Bald Soprano*. John and Doris frankly discuss their marriage which has proved a failure, but their dialogue is always couched in the third person. Although they hear and respond to each other, they do not react emotionally to each other's criticisms. The humor here has a pathetic underside, as humor focusing on failure often does.

Doris' relative who lives with them is one of those characters who makes a point by not speaking at all or only at a crucial moment. This gaunt, elderly person broods over the scene like a death's head and is perhaps the ghost of love startled into spiteful comment when John falls downstairs while escaping from his stultifying union with Doris. This may be the most successful scene in the whole play because it is trying to do only one thing, and it does it brilliantly. The dialogue is taut, and the dramatic method involving the use of the third person where one would expect the first and second is unusual for its time and would still, after the Absurdists, be highly effective. It is more original in its humor than most of the play manages to be. The allusion to the "home life of Pericles and Aspasia" is nicely ironic in its reminder of a Golden Age, but it probably would mean little to most audiences. It is merely another attempt to provide mythic veneer for the story.

John's flight from his joyless household takes him, with Lewis, into a pub for the first of two big scenes that lead up to his reunion with the masked lady and his death. Despite Johnston's adjuration that the play is not Expressionistic and should not be played that way, it would seem that this scene moves into pure Expressionism as it dramatizes John's horror and frustration at his thus-far empty life and fruitless quest. His inebriated state is suggested by endowing all the other characters with "a slight uniform swaying motion." A disconsolate flapper from an early scene turns up as a barmaid-Pandora, and from her cosmetic kit, which she drops, come the "woes of the world" in the shape of John's Nanny, a Gentleman in Black, Doubts, the Sins of the Fathers, John's own Shadow, a Clock, Minutes, and even Doris. These ghostly figures of past failures and future fears briefly create a nightmare which climaxes in a frenzied race/debate between John and his Shadow and John's attack on the clock, which interestingly enough never indicates an hour for this particular scene (though it is between two and four P.M.). Some of these figures are quite funny in their threats: "I am a Gentleman in Black. Where will you be in eternity?

There's a Hell for little children beyond the bright blue sky. And
now abideth Hate, Soap and Chastity. And the greatest of these is
Chastity'' (254).

John's Shadow reminds him that he has willed it to "grow tall
until it lay across the earth," and now his wish is granted: "I grow,
I grow with the sinking sun" (256). The Shadow is the fear of
death, a conventional bogey as well as a metaphor here for the
increasing authority and prestige of a man's mature years. John
now questions both fear of death and desire to live. "Why should I
love this thing called life?" "No reason," replies his Shadow. But
there is one: to meet once more the masked lady, to remove her
mask and fathom her mystery, to regain the ecstasy of that first
revelation. But what man can outrun Death, he asks. As a Fury-like
chorus of Minutes torments him, John flings himself on the clock
to destroy the thief that is robbing him of life. This is one of the
most theatrical scenes in the play. Certainly, if *Bride* owes anything
to Goethe's *Faust,* as has been suggested, this Walpurgisnacht in
the pub is part of such a debt.

In scene ix (four P.M.), John is found guilty of a misdemeanor
for attacking the clock and is sentenced to jail and a fine. However,
he is immediately released for military service. Scene x (seven P.M.),
interestingly called "The Scythe and the Sunset" (a title Johnston
was to use years later for what is probably his best play since the
Thirties), shows John as a soldier on active service at the front. His
age is not quite clear. When he says that "schoolboys come back
into their own" during wartime, he is probably being more ironic
than literal. However, the schoolboy in him is apparent when he
exclaims, "Start the drums again and let us get on with the War so I
can use my bayonet on somebody" (271).

To judge from their roles, the companions are somewhat older
than John here. The scenes apparently do not follow him chronologically through his life. At times, he seems old in situations that
must have occurred fairly early; here he seems young in a scene
near the end of the play and the end of his life. The point is that he
is both young and old; youth and age coexist in him simultaneously
to imply the brevity of his life from the point of view of the Ultimate Observer in Time Two.

Although scene x can be ironic in its treatment of war, the main
point is the encounter with Egbert who, more than ever before,
seems to speak for the Ultimate Observer. Egbert is briefly the
enemy whom John stalks with fixed bayonet, but soon they are

singing the old school song together. However, Egbert actually wishes to die, to be killed. To John's comment that "Sensible people don't want to die," Egbert replies that "Everybody wants to die. Only they usually don't know it" (274). Autumn, sunset, sleep — all seem good to Egbert, for they suggest conclusion and death. "To sleep? Perhaps never to wake," John counters with some fear. But who would want life without death, joy without pain, Egbert replies. John himself has already given this answer to Doris in the proposal scene: "The magic of happiness is that it must have beginning and ending" (222). This is a part of the bond we sign with Time, Egbert reminds him, and John agrees that life would indeed have been worth it if there were only time for one thing more: another glimpse of "the face that granted me that brief half minute of true immortality." However, anything that has happened or has existed, including that brief interval with the masked lady (i.e., his glimpse into Time Two), exists still and is not so much to be repeated as perhaps rejoined in that other dimension.

The music imagery in this scene harks back to the Prelude. Perhaps life is "nothing but a tune played by somebody upon a piano," suggests Egbert. The notes of music are John's life in Time One; they require annotation to be brought into being. Having been once heard, they exist in an eternity, not as a line with beginning and end, but as an entity in space which may be viewed *in toto* from Time Two. This is what Egbert is trying to teach John.

It is interesting to note here that John refuses to kill Egbert because he knows him; Egbert is "someone in particular," not a stranger. There is a similarity here with the scene in *The Moon in the Yellow River* in which Dobelle refuses to participate in revenge by helping Tausch report Lanigan for the murder of Darrell Blake. Just as Dobelle's refusal to cooperate with Tausch is his way of saying "no" to further violence for the sake of an idea, so in a similar way John learns that everybody is someone in particular and refuses to kill Egbert, dramatically bringing the war to a close.

The peace conference is instituted at eleven P.M. with the companions as negotiators. John appears in the midst of these proceedings mourning his lost bride. The Bust is also present, and John pleads with him for a reunion with his bride before he dies. It is late — nearly midnight — but in the manner of Strindberg's mummy in *The Ghost Sonata,* the Bust stops time by stopping the pendulum of the clock as it is about to strike twelve, the hour of death. As the music of the Prelude is heard, the masked lady reappears. John

passionately reminds her that on "the first day of my life" they
were lovers. To her he owes all; to her he will give all — for one
glimpse of her face. She nods, turns her back to the audience and
unmasks, at which a "thrill of horror runs through everybody
upon the stage." For John, it is the revelation he has waited for
most of his life. It is Death he has loved and Death he now
embraces, but as he does, the figure collapses into thin air, and he
falls dead. It only remains to honor the fallen hero in the coda with
a hymn to Adonis.

VII *Music*

In *Bride,* music is almost as important as character and is "inti-
mately connected with the plot," according to Johnston. First,
there is the "cold wintry" theme music with which the orchestra
begins and which is taken up by the piano players, He and She.
This is the music of Time Two, and it is heard again at the end of
the play to establish a link between the time of the Prelude and the
time to which John succeeds on his death. The variety of music that
follows is amazing; it is no wonder Johnston called his play a musical, which it is in a somewhat restricted sense. There are marches,
hymns, choruses, carols, school songs, ballads, dances, and popular tunes performed by individuals, small groups, "semi-
choruses," choruses, a statue and a radio, in addition to the orchestra in the pit. There are also piano duets and piano and violin solos.
The function of music may be to present or restate theme (here
time, as in the "wintry" music), to comment ironically ("Sumer is
icumen in"), to celebrate ("Sing, oh children of triumphant
Zeus"), to mourn ("Woe, woe, Adonis is dead!"), to join in marriage (a traditional wedding march), to mock ("Cuckoo!
Cuckoo!"), to satirize ("Ready, aye, ready"), to introduce ("First
from the North comes mighty Hercules"), to contrast (the dance
with the theme music in scene xi), to toast ("For he's a jolly good
fellow"), and to worship ("My beloved spake and said unto me").

VIII *In Conclusion*

A Bride for the Unicorn is a play that warrants study, both for its
weaknesses which are instructive and its strengths which are
impressive. It is the child of a magnificent imagination and one of
the most ambitious plays in modern drama, although it fails as

often as it succeeds. The structure is imaginative but too complex. There are too many mythic levels, too many allusions that do not last beyond the moment, too much superfluous dialogue, too many songs, and too much demanded of the music. Characterization is not effective; John Foss, like the masked lady, remains throughout an abstraction, while a character like the Bust has too many sides to his personality — Lynceus, He (the gentleman in the dressing gown), tippler companion to the schoolboys, Ultimate Observer, musician — to register strongly enough in any one of them. Although Johnston felt that an audience might not be ready for his theme of death as a logical and desirable culmination of life, one suspects that viewers less baffled by his use of myth, allegory, and a complex chronology might have been brought around to consider, if not accept, an unfamiliar theme. At one time, *Bride* was his favorite play, and he has expressed regret that it was published too soon and in a form that he now dislikes. It does exist in at least one other version, however, and perhaps with Johnston's penchant for reworking his plays, it will sometime emerge in a more viable form.

CHAPTER 4

The Romance of Aran:
Storm Song

I   "... Sybil Thorndyke marooned in a lighthouse"

CONSIDERING the nature of Johnston's first three plays, it
seemed a two-to-one chance that his fourth play would be
"experimental" along the lines of either *The Old Lady Says "No!"*
and *A Bride for the Unicorn,* or barring that, at least a return to the
poetic realism of *The Moon in the Yellow River.* What was not
expected was the rather ordinary little romantic comedy called
Storm Song (1934) that could only be, as Johnston himself was to
call it, "a sad little attempt at the popular market."[1] It is easy to be
critical of this innocuous piece of commercial playwriting, for it
made no demands on its creator, its actors, or its audience. On
paper, the characters are drawn without much depth or dimension,
although a company like the Gate may have brought the play to
some degree of life. It may be indicative that when Johnston published the play in 1935, he provided a set of character sketches that
say more about the characters than the play does. The themes are
obvious and remain relatively unexplored. Moreover, they were not
problems that seemed especially to engage Johnston, then or later.

Storm Song depicts the conflict between a young film editor who
is (or will be) a genuine artist and an older movie pioneer of substantial reputation but dedicated to a highly personal and somewhat passé style of film-making. The conflict is complicated, but
not to any great extent, by the young man's romantic interest which
brings him to the moment of choice: love or art. All of this is familiar enough, for there are many variations on the theme. The prob-

74

lem here is that the older man's personality dominates much of the first two acts which really go nowhere.

On the other hand, the romantic theme is more exciting when we hear about it than when we see the lovers together. And worst of all, the love affair is a means, not of forcing the young man to a significant choice between making films and making love, but merely of characterizing the girl as so noble and self-sacrificing that the young man is spared the trouble of having to make a choice. It is, finally, rather bland fare even with most of the ingredients for a popular success: some bright dialogue, a "serious" theme that was also popular, some curious local color, an exotic setting, potentially theatrical characters, and the subject of movie-making that in 1934 had an aura of glamour about it.

II *On Location: Drame à Clef*

Storm Song grew out of an invitation extended to Johnston by the American film director Robert Flaherty to watch the making of a documentary film on the Aran Islands which lie thirty miles off the western coast of Ireland in Galway Bay. In 1931, Flaherty decided to turn his cameras on the fisherfolk whom John Synge had celebrated in *The Aran Islands* and in his one-act play, *Riders to the Sea.* The film-maker had first heard of the Islands on a trans-atlantic crossing when an Irishman, aroused by stories of the tribulations of the American Depression, told of an island people whose lives were so hard they had to make their own soil by carrying seaweed up rugged shores and mixing it with sand. The director was impressed by the story, and in January, 1932, began work on the film which was called *Man of Aran* and is one of the most famous documentaries in film history and Flaherty's third feature-length work. Since *Man of Aran* was to be a "film poem," the director was not interested in story as such but in "inventing a myth of a folk way of life which would apply to people all over the world."[2] The film was to center about two principal motifs: the everyday life on the islands and the terrible autumnal storms that attack from the open Atlantic with an almost unnatural fury. The landing of a curragh (an island canoe) during one such storm is the climax of Flaherty's film; in *Storm Song,* the project of bringing in the fishing nets in a stormy sea is the offstage climax.

One of the best features of Johnston's play is his portrait of a director, Szilard, modeled on Flaherty, who is totally committed to perfecting his art in his own highly personal style. The other main character, Gordon King, is modeled on a young university man, John Goldman, who, unlike King, had already studied film in the Soviet Union and returned with definite views about film editing. The conflict between director and editor as dramatized in the first two acts of the play evidently characterized the relationship of Flaherty and Goldman. Nothing of a theorist, Flaherty was an intuitive artist, not only with the camera but in the way he went about cutting a film once it was shot. He was led by his camera in the same way some authors are led by their headstrong characters. Goldman thought Flaherty had a fine sense of rhythm for whatever and whomever he photographed but not much sense of the rhythm of a completed film. Thus, the conflict between Johnston's two characters, Szilard and Gordon King, like their real-life counterparts, stems from a disagreement over the editing. Szilard tries to make the completed film in the camera, the way Flaherty worked. Goldman recalled an example of Flaherty's prodigality with film in which he used up a complete magazine (two hundred feet) in one unbroken shot which ranged over the perpendicular walls of a cliff from the top down to the sea and back again. Such expenditures of film and effort came from his desire "to do it all *in and through* the camera."[3]

Johnston employed this incident as the basis for a confrontation between his two characters. Goldman finally realized that the director was shooting the same things repeatedly. Knowing he could edit a good film (*Man of Aran* is approximately seventy-six minutes long) from the footage they had, he prompted the producer to call a halt to further shooting. A similar situation precipitates tension in the play when Szilard is denied more film by his producer. *Man of Aran* opened in London on April 25, 1934. It was not well received in England but fared somewhat better in America. Even though the British did not officially enter it in the Venice Film Festival, it was awarded the Grand Prix. Johnston's play which it had inspired opened almost three months *earlier* at Dublin's Gate Theatre. This might indicate something of the haste with which the whole project of the play was undertaken.

III   *Plot and Characters*

The plot of *Storm Song,* such as it is, involves a film company on location on a barren island, near the end of its budget, its schedule, and its patience. Waiting for the autumn storms that will provide the natural drama for the climactic moments of the film, the company plays host briefly to a collection of types ranging from an accountant, a cynical film critic, a flabby specimen of local aristocracy, a folk music enthusiast, and two reasonably attractive women, one of whom has an affair with the young would-be genius who is editing the film under the thumb of the dictatorial director. The director dies filming his storm sequence; boy and girl, who have been living together, attend the opening in London where (a) the film is a success, (b) he gets offers to edit and eventually direct for Solberg, the producer (perhaps inspired by Irving Thalberg or Samuel Goldwyn or both), and (c) he is admitted to the State Institute of Cinema in Moscow where he may *not* bring the girl. Now the choice: love or art? Johnston's ending would be unsatisfactory for a really serious play, for the young man's decision is made under the mistaken impression that the girl is tired of him and about to leave anyway. She knows she cannot compete with cinema and courageously misleads him, causing him to take the opportunity to go to Moscow. Certainly there is nothing realistic or even believable about the denouement, but in this kind of play it really makes little difference. Johnston was never deeply involved in the proceedings.

Such interest as the play still has centers on (a) the rather quaint portrait of a young movie industry, (b) the *drame à clef* technique, and (c) the relationship of the two central characters, Szilard and Gordon King, which deserves some further comment. Szilard (named, as Johnston has explained, after Leo Szilard, the noted physicist and authority in nuclear research whom the playwright happened to meet on a transatlantic crossing) gets his temperament from his Hungarian ancestry and his early experience in film from an American education on a movie lot. At the same time that his camera work has brought him fame and his personality notoriety, Szilard's lack of discipline has reduced him to working on his own projects when he can cajole money from production heads whom he has not yet alienated. He has no idea he is creating "Art"; he has no patience with theorists and dilettantes whom he would group together. Szilard has convinced himself that pure photography is all and that cutting is hack work. His documentary films have "extraordinary power and beauty," but their detractors are as numerous as his enemies. He worships his work and the Picture, and he pursues both with an obsessed energy. The director has no trouble establishing contact with the simple, even primitive people whom he views in the lenses of his camera, but he is a bully to his other associates. He projects a celluloid charm and manipulates his rich backers with cunning. Szilard fights with young King because he sees in him qualities he knows he himself lacks; for the same reason, he respects and admires the younger man.

That Gordon King has personality and charisma must be taken on his own word; that he has genius must be taken on Johnston's, for King does not noticeably demonstrate any of these qualities in the play. His redeeming feature is his admiration for Szilard who is "in many ways his spiritual father," but he contradicts and disagrees with most of what the older man stands for in film-making.[4] Because Szilard is something of a tyrant and King is proud and hostile toward him, their relationship is characterized by tension and temper. The young man recognizes in Szilard's photography a quality that is worth whatever effort he as editor can expend on it, but with the ruthlessness of the young, King is quite willing to subvert what he knows to be the director's goal to his own theories and ideas about the final print.

Act I is mostly expository. Act II gets to the point very effectively in dramatizing the secondary theme of youth vs. maturity, the intuitive vs. the intellectual, and the pioneer vs. the second generation. "He's our theorist," Szilard says condescendingly of his young editor. "His idea is that moving pictures should be made with a scenario and a pair of scissors" (67). The initial conflict between the director and young King is built around the episode Goldman described in which Szilard spent two hundred feet of film in an unbroken shot of the face of a cliff without ever showing the skyline. Gordon edits the film according to his own ideas, using some "cheat shots" and close-ups. "You can't get any impression of the real height of those cliffs from straight photography," he insists; "It has to be treated or it is meaningless" (55). When the director sees the edited version of his long shot, he explodes: "You and your wipes and your fades and your lap dissolves! Had Chaplin any of these? Do you suppose Griffith ever wanted them? But that's all you've got nowadays. Stunts, stunts, stunts!" (76–77).

In the first scene of Act III, Johnston turns to the matter of dramatizing Szilard's ability to mesmerize the islanders into cooperating with him even if conditions make it extremely hazardous to do so. This very real danger to the actors becomes a launching point for a return to the original conflict between the two men.

New here, however, is the theme of the higher reality of art vs. the simple reality of raw photography. If Szilard has shot some "great stuff" in the months on the islands, it will still be only a "cameraman's picture" which nobody will believe; it will be so real it will not only be assumed to be fake but will look as though it has not been faked very well.

Szilard insists that he will fulfill his big opportunity to make a "full, true, authentic record, with nothing shirked or nothing left unsaid," a "High Art Quota Picture" that will not be a popular success but will be "the like of which nobody has ever seen before" (116). Out of affection for the native actors and pride in his undertaking, he wants to make a film of complete integrity. The director dismisses Gordon's charge that in doing so he "will have drowned half a dozen Islanders," adding scornfully that King may stay with his girl (instead of assisting in filming the final storm sequence) if he wishes, but "remember when she lets you down that work never lets you down, if you stick to it." These are his last words to Gordon, and we learn later that he is drowned while filming during the storm.

In the disappointing final scene, Gordon, inspired by Szilard's defiance of the storm, completes the film in the way the director himself would have done. Szilard had wanted pure reality, and that is finally the quality of the film: nothing is faked. The picture is a success but for the wrong reason: it is advertised as "The Last Gesture of a Giant." It is a commercial success because it is "the picture that drowned Szilard." This is the major irony of the play: the director's death was necessary to make a commercial success of a noncommercial film. There is the further irony that this most commercial of Johnston's plays is itself an indictment of commercialism.[5]

The play is vitiated in its last scene because the dynamic center, Szilard, is missing. King's romantic interest, Jal Joyce, recognizes that she is no match for his obsession with film and so bows out without a fight, a capitulation that would not seem typical of her character. Gordon then can say "I told you so" for Szilard: "He said you'd let me down." And he is off to Moscow and bigger things.

Storm Song is not a bad play, merely an insignificant one; more was expected from a man of Johnston's talent at this particular juncture in his career. It seems that he temporarily abandoned experimentation to acquiesce to the demands of the commercial theater by courting a public that was clearly fascinated by the mystique of the movies. Although he has included *Storm Song* in the recently published volume I of his *Dramatic Works,* there seems no reason to revise his own verdict of 1954 that it was "more of a burp than a song."[6]

CHAPTER 5

A Conscience for Society:
The Golden Cuckoo

I *Portrait of a Rebel*

*T*HE *Golden Cuckoo* premiered at the Gate Theatre in April, 1939. After the lapse of *Storm song*, Johnston's fifth play is a return to the single most important theme running through his work: rebellion. In this respect, *Cuckoo* is the third of four plays (*The Old Lady, The Moon,* and *The Scythe and the Sunset*) dealing with this theme; these four represent Johnston's best work for the theater. His first two plays deal with the violence of revolution by focusing on individual rebels as members of larger movements (e.g., the Republicans or Emmet's followers); in *The Golden Cuckoo,* however, the rebellion is solely a one-man affair. Though an attack is made on the government, it is not politically oriented; thus, this is the least "Irish" of the four plays.

Like the others, *Cuckoo* is a "history play" about a real person who undertook his own one-man revolution and was declared insane for his trouble. It is a tribute to a man who reacted with understandable vigor when his society denied him justice of the most elementary sort. All this is hardly to the credit of a society that then made the rebel into a *rara avis* for his symbolic act and finally ousted him altogether. The tragedy here is not that many revolted to no end but that one man stood alone in just defiance of governmental authority. Although ultimately serious, *The Golden Cuckoo* is a mellow, humorous play whose rebel is a metaphor for visionaries and all slightly aberrant citizens.

81

It all began, according to Johnston, on a Monday night in May, 1926, when Francis Walter Louis Alphonsus Doheny, in order to provoke a trial by jury, charged the windows of a small post office in Kilkenny, aiming to damage government property to the modest sum of about five pounds. His assault was complete with his personal flag, a martial slogan, and his own "Rational Anthem." This civil disturbance seems to have originated out of what Johnston calls "a sense of the injustice of life," rather than an understandable animus toward the quality of the postal service. Doheny was captured without difficulty and led away into custody singing his Anthem (to the tune of "Come Back to Erin"). Doheny had expected — in fact, had intended — to provoke a short jail sentence to dramatize his particular frustration with life, but he was utterly nonplused to find that a humane and enlightened judge decided that the question of the injustices of his life was subordinate to his sanity and sentenced him in July of 1926 to three months in a mental institution. From his place of confinement, Doheny addressed a protest to members of the Irish bar in the form of a description of his revolt written in the third person; it was this account that interested Johnston and remained with him until he wrote the play some dozen years later.[1]

Ordinarily the tale would have ended there, with Doheny serving out his term in an asylum and hopefully taking his lesson to heart. But in 1956, two years after Johnston published *The Golden Cuckoo,* he received a letter from Doheny, then an inmate in an asylum in Thomastown, County Kilkenny, requesting a copy of the play. Johnston, who had never met Doheny, was surprised to hear he was alive thirty years after the event that had brought him to his attention and responded, writing the old man that he was deeply moved by the injustice to him and that his defiant attack on the post office seemed "in many ways to parallel the events of 1916."[2] There was no reply.

II   *The Anti-Functionalist*

However sympathetically Johnston responded to Doheny's act of defiance and however reasonable he found the old man's expectation of a brief jail term instead of a stay in a mental institution, when he came to dramatize the incident, he found it necessary to create his fictional character, Professor Dotheright, as a man who is eccentric enough that society views him condescendingly.

Dotheright's occasional occupation (writing obituaries), his living quarters (a partially converted stable), his associates (the salty-tongued kleptomaniac, Mrs. Vanderbilt), his incidental employment ("During the academic year I escort very small children to their schools, and in some cases I have been known to do their more difficult sums for them in return for a modest weekly gratuity.") — all coalesce into a portrait of a man who is hardly the community's average citizen. He is, in fact, a variation of the simpleton who calls social values into question with a naivete that at first astonishes and then alienates.

But Professor Dotheright is really not one of "society's cranks" as much as he is "society's conscience."[3] If society were truly concerned with giving him his rights, it would have to reexamine itself, redefine its priorities, and perhaps even revolt. But society does not respond kindly or even fairly to outsiders who threaten the status quo; it is better to get rid of them or to "fix" the situation. This response Johnston defines as Functionalism, and it is this philosophy, he argues, that most societies live by, unwittingly creating the martyrs of the future. As the "prevailing philosophy of the day," it is based on a distrust of the word "What" and a high regard for the word "How."

The ultimate criterion for all questions is not What is it? but How does it operate? What is true is what works: what is untrue is what fails to work. The most telling thing that we can say about Crime is that it doesn't pay.

In the absence of a moral law — the supreme What? — we tend to concern ourselves only with the question, How will it deliver the goods? And as nothing really delivers the goods, except in a most temporary way, we have been driven to the lamentable conclusion that nothing is really true.[4]

Johnston has taken Doheny as a model for his only character in the play who places a higher value on the "What" than on the "How." His Professor Dotheright is the "anti-Functionalist," the innocent, the saint, the redeemer of at least some of the other characters, and, of course, the martyr. As the "What" man, he is the only one who demonstrates morality through an examination of the event. Dotheright stands in contrast to the other characters who blindly succumb to the conventional answers and responses most ethical situations evoke. His humanity is complete throughout the play; his one lapse — an insistence that an obituary be published whether or not the subject is dead — is corrected immediately. He demands only what he has been promised for the completed work, neither more nor less than he is entitled to. Dotheright is a quiet moral rock in a restless sea of immoral uncertainty and compromise. His speeches reveal a reserve and sense of security that place him in a different moral league than the others even when he is threatened. But without taking anything away from his hero, Johnston uses secondary characters to precipitate the conflict with the law and, at the end of the play, to show that Dotheright's gesture of defiance has not, after all, failed.

III   Plot and Characters

The Golden Cuckoo follows the general outline of the dramatic confrontation between Mr. Doheny and the law. Having been refused payment of one pound, six shillings and eightpence for an obituary, Professor Dotheright is unable to pay his share of a cab fare and is encouraged by the driver, Mr. Hooley, and a fellow passenger, Mr. Penniwise, to make an issue of the small debt. When a reasonable appeal to the editor of the paper fails, Dotheright dramatizes the injustice by interrupting a radio broadcast commemorating historic revolts by breaking the windows of the nearby post office and attempting to occupy it. When all concerned in the proceeding are hailed into court (Lettie Lowe, the editor's daughter and an actress of uncertain talent; her newscaster lover, Wynstan Chaplain; her reporter husband, Paddy Golightly; and, of course, the cab driver and the fellow passenger, Penniwise), they extricate themselves by blaming Professor Dotheright, feeling they have done him a good turn by getting him off, not with the jail term he wanted, but with a short sentence in an insane asylum. He is appalled that his sincere attempt to challenge the law has been interpreted as insanity, and even though Lettie tries to arrange his bond, he rejects her attempt and returns willingly to the asylum, disillusioned but with his integrity intact, even as his saintliness is certified by a miracle borrowed from Shaw's *St. Joan.*

To draw lines clearly between the protagonist and his principal detractors, Johnston resorts, somewhat in the manner of *A Bride for the Unicorn,* to tag names. Professor Dotheright (pronounced Duthery) is then Mr. Do-the-right. The vulgar and realistically dishonest newspaper editor who is both "a smiling wheedler" and "a roaring bully" is Mr. Lowd, and the flighty actress and her "arid" reporter-husband are Mr. and Mrs. Golightly. Her unctuous newscaster lover is Chaplain who, as high priest of the news media,

seduces his listeners into simple-minded acceptance with his minis-
terial tones. The other passenger in the cab, Penniwise, has with
foolish frugality given up love and poetry for the lowly post of
solicitor's clerk. Mrs. Vanderbilt, the thieving old harridan who
keeps Dotheright's stable apartment for him, recognizes the irony
in her own name when she explains that her late husband had "out-
landish connections." The judge who can be "fixed" is named
Bland; and worst of all, the subject of the obituary is Mr. Boddy.
All this might suggest that they are more characters than people,
and this is true except for Dotheright. However, proper allowances
should be made for the nature of the play itself. It is usually called a
farce, but it should be added that it is a farce that turns serious,
even pathetic, at the end without detracting from its basically
humorous nature. Johnston describes it as "a very serious play"
which might very likely "go off the rails if allowed to betray the
fact that it considers itself to be the slightest farcical."[5] With a
player like the great Cyril Cusack in the central role, it is not hard
to imagine why this can be called Johnston's "funniest play, and
his tenderest."[6]

IV   *The Cuckoo's Rebellion*

The first references to Mr. Dotheright foreshadow society's
treatment of him: to Lettie Lowe, he is merely an object — an old
man who "goes with" the stable apartment she has just bought as a
love nest. His fate is clear when Chaplain, her lover, replies, reflect-
ing society's usual disposition toward odd folk, that she'll "have to
get rid of him." When Dotheright enters, he has a hunted look and
is already aware that he is the prey. His complete failure — or
refusal — to understand the offer of a loan for cab fare is the first
indication that he has an independence and integrity so unique as to
make him an outcast. The story of the premature obituary and the
newspaper's refusal to pay for it leads into the Professor's Declara-
tion of Independence: "All my life I have found it impossible to
meet with dishonesty and injustice and keep a civil tongue in my
head."[7]

Hooley, the cab driver, is also the victim of an injustice; he was,
he says, in the Post Office in 1916 (during the Easter Week Rebellion) and because of crookedness and rascality got only a medal, no
pension. Dotheright asks his advice as a "resolute man" regarding
his treatment by the newspaper. "Go back and kick up hell,"

Hooley tells him, but Penniwise, Grattan-like, suggests reasonable discussion. The choice is clear as it always is in Johnston's plays of civil rebellion: "You see, gentlemen," says Dotheright, "we have here two conflicting points of view — the constitutional and the revolutionary. Which of them is right?" He chooses the peaceful "constitutional" approach and decides to confront Lowd.

Johnston describes Lowd as a "crook with a conscience" who justifies everything he does in terms of realistic commonsense. He merely counters Dotheright's demand for payment with an offer of another assignment at a slightly higher figure to cover both pieces of work. But now it is not a matter of money; it is a matter of integrity. Dotheright discovers that he is "a contributor of little importance" to a newspaper that regards him as expendable. He charges that it is "inconsistent" for a firm to pay so much for public relations and refuse to pay a legal debt of one pound, six shillings and eightpence. This is a word at which the editor balks. Here Lowd is at his best as an exponent of Functionalism: if Dotheright will demonstrate that he is a person of importance, he will be treated accordingly. But to Lowd, a man's worth depends upon his productivity and nothing more. And "nothing," he might have said with King Lear, "will come of nothing." To be consistent then, he will pay Dotheright only according to his worth and importance: namely, nothing. His first approach having failed, it remains for the Professor to undertake the "second Phase" and resort to the law.

Dotheright discovers, however, that the law is not for "unimportant people"; his lawyer has been promptly "fixed" by Lowd before the Professor can see him. There is clearly no course left but to undertake some kind of dramatic revolt against the system to draw attention to the injustice. The ideal opportunity comes when Mrs. Graves, a cabinet minister's wife, is dedicating a plaque commemorating heroes of Ireland's rebellions. Chaplain is there to report the event and introduce the lady with an appropriate quote from Thomas Jefferson: "A Rebellion now and then is a good thing. . . ." But of course, nobody really believes this; it is acceptable doctrine only when applied to the safe past where dead heroes are no embarrassment to the living who eulogize them. As Mrs. Graves begins to extoll "a free land where the rule of law guarantees the right and liberties of even the humblest," Dotheright takes exception to "the ridiculous proposition that the rule of law guarantees us anything" (31). Hooley reminds him that there is only "one virtue that matters, and it's Courage. We learnt that when we occupied the Post Office."

So that is what Dotheright decides to do: occupy the post office in the name of Injustice which is "the supreme sin — not in those who commit it, but in those who submit to it." With the stale rhetoric of political oratory that F.E. Cummings parodied so effectively in "next to of course god america i love you," Mrs. Graves has just inquired of her radio audience: "Where are the young men ... who would march out into the streets and proclaim in arms the truths for which we stood? Where are the men of '41, of '89, of '98, of '48 — the men of 1916?" (33). The immediate answer comes from a determined Dotheright who proposes to "hold a Rebellion" and invites others to join, assuring them that the days of heroism Mrs. Graves has been praising are not over. He proposes a sovereign republic with a slogan of "One Truth, One Law, One Justice" and a flag that is a part of the post office awning. And what right has he to proclaim a republic? The same right as anybody else, he replies.

Of course, all this is a careful parody of Irish politics: the windy declaiming of Mrs. Graves, Dotheright's proclamation of a republic, the empty memorial to the dead past, the celebration of past rebellions, and the rejection of the rebels by the man in the street. An irritated postmistress baptizes the new head of state with water from the upstairs window, and the rebellion is under way with the assault on the post office window. But Dotheright finds that he stands alone in occupying government property; the rallying cry of Mrs. Graves is not answered as it was in 1916. It is a one-man rebellion by the uncommon man, and in a parody of Hamlet's plea to "report me and my cause aright," he is hauled away. Throughout this scene, the actress, who never had a chance to play Ophelia, distributes flowers and herbs through the crowd in a parody of Shakespeare's heroine, thus introducing the motif of madness, the charge that will bring down the government of the Professor's one-man republic. Johnston is usually subtle and witty in his use of music for irony or satire but never more than here, when a radio, accidentally knocked over, blares forth Wagner's *Parsifal,* a musical celebration of the guileless fool (*"der reine Tor"*) who graduated from shooting swans to protecting the Holy Grail.

Act III restates the play's theme that society deals with its cuckoos by restraining them: the word "fix" continually recurs. The actress has been able to fix matters so that Judge Bland will hear their case. The damages will be paid ("fixed") by those caught up in the net with Dotheright. Golightly, the reporter, manages to get his wife away before the police arrive; her reputation is saved, and she and her husband can safely attend to fixing matters for the others. Everything and everybody, in fact, is fixed except Mr. Dotheright whose demands must now be satisfied or the newspaper will be drawn into a scandal as a result of all the publicity. Only the actress realizes that if Dotheright is fixed, the whole episode will become meaningless and absurd. At one point it seems that the Professor has indeed given in, for Lowd explains that he has fixed him by arranging things with his "wife." Mrs. Vanderbilt, pretending to be Mrs. Dotheright, has taken money, promising to fix everything with her "husband." But Dotheright is not fixed, nor is he any longer interested in the money *per se:* "Why cannot people understand that what we have done is ... for humanity — and in obedience to our voices" (42).

The references to "voices" is Johnston's tribute to Shaw's *St. Joan.* Dotheright is presented as the visionary betrayed, not by his voices, but like Joan, by those who are deaf to the promptings of moral passion. In an unexpected turn, which seems to be Johnston's only obvious contrivance, Mr. Boddy, the subject of the unpublished obituary, suddenly and unaccountably dies; Lowd is called on to answer questions since he not only anticipated the death by ordering the premature obituary but is also in a position to profit from it. Both he and Boddy had financial interests in "chemical manure," and a false rumor of Boddy's death would have permitted Lowd to buy up stock at a low rate, all of which points to a breach of ethics. Moreover, Boddy was also involved with explosives, a fact interesting to a government accustomed to frequent internal dissension. Johnston's too-obvious moral here is that involvement with "manure" of any kind may lead to an explosive situation, for Lowd is forced to resign.

In the climax of the play, Dotheright's betrayers explain to him how lucky he is that the judge let him off with a short sentence in the asylum since he was not responsible for his action. He is appalled at the suggestion that he is not responsible — that he is, in fact, insane: "He spoke of insanity and you did not deny it?" They have undone him by pleading too well. Like Shaw's Joan, he cries out, "But my voices — my voices? Do they not want my — my services?" It seems not. The betrayal by men, he tells Mrs. Golightly, is no longer important; there is something more terrible than that, for men and women can forgive each other. "But when the Lord Himself chooses to mock His servants, who is there to forgive Him?" (46). This is the most terrible — and serious — point in the play: the moment of Dotheright's overwhelming disillusionment with God. For a saint, nothing could be worse. It is reminiscent of the scene in *St. Joan* just before she agrees to sign her recantation.

V   *"How long, O Lord"*

In the denouement that has parallels with Shaw's Epilogue in which Joan reappears in 1923, the principals gather a few weeks later in response to Lettie's invitation. There are some changes; the saint's courage has become contagious for some of those unwittingly involved in the rebellion. Penniwise has persuaded the postmistress, Miss Peering, his love of many years before, to marry him. They will settle in the post office where he will write poetry as he always wanted. Hooley, splendid in a new cabman's uniform, has gotten his pension plus payment in arrears. Lettie, the flighty actress, has begun to see through her vapid newscaster, and Paddy Golightly, her husband, seems a little less like second-best. The point of the gathering, she explains, is to ask them all to put up bond to free Dotheright.

All of them refuse, sounding like Joan's colleagues who claimed that if she returned to earth (and as a saint she could) she would only be an embarrassment to them, and the Church would probably burn her again. Only Lowd, no longer editor, can be cajoled by his daughter into contributing money; she reminds him that although it is inconsistent to pay for nothing, he has had satisfaction because Dotheright had been put away for a time. When the Professor appears, however, he rejects their money and the freedom it would bring, asking only to return "home" to the asylum. But it is a subversion of justice for him to be there, objects the actress. "Justice is of little importance when you know that you have been right," he replies. At her exclamation of "Heavens above," he reminds them that he has offered his services to Heaven and his proposal has been ignored. "If Heaven does not choose to pay its debts..., I have nothing more to say" (53).

To Lettie's exclamation that he is a saint, he replies that he has tested this possibility by attempting "some simple miracle" but without success. Therefore, "As a Saint, I am a failure. But as a Madman — ah, there at least, I am in the forefront of the field" (53). However, this Golden Cuckoo has misunderstood the silence of Heaven, and in the last moments of the play there is a celestial response. Heaven's bluff has been called by asking for a miracle; one comes as Dotheright makes a sign of benediction over the reunited Golightlys: an egg from the "rooster" in the stable loft falls on Paddy's head and gently breaks. In the first scene of the play, Dotheright had insisted that the fowl was a hen, despite the fact that it crowed. "You'll never get an egg out of that," Penniwise had told him. But the egg comes, signifying Heaven's seal of approval on the Professor's saintliness. He is too good for this earth, and Heaven has wisely placed him in a special situation apart from common men, an asylum in the original sense of the word which he himself recognizes as his true home. Along with Shaw's Joan, who had her own share of good luck with poultry, Dotheright might be heard to wonder when the beautiful land of Ireland will be ready to receive its saints. "How long, O Lord, how long?"

This is a wise and gentle play, utterly lacking in the drama and violence of Johnston's other plays of rebellion. It makes the point that free men have a right openly to defy their government when their personal rights are challenged and legal recourse is exhausted. In Johnston's plays of revolt, such action is exceptional. Too often in Ireland's history, simplistic if well-meant rebellion preceded the "constitutional" approach, undercutting efforts to achieve justice through diplomacy and negotiations. *The Golden Cuckoo* still has much to say regarding the human spirit and the obligations of a government in a democratic society.

CHAPTER 6

An Irish Morality:
The Dreaming Dust

I *The Subject of Swift*

JOHNSTON'S seventh work for the theater is a curious and exciting play based on documented facts and highly probable theories about the life of Jonathan Swift. The full story of Johnston's interest in Swift as a subject for the theater covers more than two decades. It begins with his reactions to two other Irish plays about Swift and does not conclude until the publication in 1960 of the final version of *The Dreaming Dust* in the collected plays. In 1930, W. B. Yeats gave the Abbey Theatre *The Words Upon the Window Pane* which centers on a séance in which a medium calls up the spirits of Swift and Vanessa, much as the actors call into life the Swift circle in *The Dreaming Dust*. Yeats' short play provides an answer to one of the principal enigmas of Dublin's Dean of St. Patrick's Cathedral: why he refused to marry Vanessa. "I have something in my blood no child must inherit," he tells her through the voice of the medium. This is a direct reference to his suspicion of madness which may also both cause and reflect a general pessimism concerning mankind.

Lord Edward Longford, the patron and partner of MacLiammoir and Edwards in their Gate Theatre, wrote a play called *Yahoo* in 1933 which made no pretense of being historically accurate in its portrait of Swift and the two women in his life.[1] In Longford's play, Swift is an old man embittered by neglect who takes out his venom by writing *Gulliver's Travels*. *Yahoo* is a superficial portrait that explains little about Swift, including his failure to marry: it

91

was just that, like Hamlet, he "lacked advancement" ("I was poor") and did not have good health. Longford arranges a secret marriage between Swift and Stella for the sole purpose of allowing the Dean to outwit Vanessa, but the reason for secrecy is not clear. Johnston may very well have noted with interest Longford's use of the near-quotation ("I am what I am") from Shakespeare's Sonnet CXXI which also occurs at the end of *The Dreaming Dust*. It was apparently *Yahoo* that most fascinated Johnston and led him to extend what was practically a Swiftian tradition in Irish drama. He first produced a radio script for the BBC in 1938 entitled *Weep for Polyphemus*. *The Dreaming Dust* in an early version followed two years later, premiering on March 25, 1940 at the Gate Theatre.

The research that Johnston had done for these projects was reflected in a long article for the *Dublin Historical Record* in 1941,[2] which later grew to book length and, with full documentation, appeared as *In Search of Swift* (1959). In the meantime, there had been other versions of the play, the final version appearing in the collected plays. In addition, a television production was entitled, after the radio play, *Weep for the Cyclops*.

A prime difficulty in the composition of *The Dreaming Dust* stemmed from the necessity of dealing with "a set of characters actually taken from life, the oddness of whose conduct is inescapable, whatever their real motives may have been."[3] Moreover, even the facts of the lives of Swift, Stella, and Vanessa were difficult to establish. As Johnston worked his way through Swiftian scholarship, he was amazed at the number of inaccuracies of long standing that could be noted quite easily. For example, the plaque with Swift's epitaph in St. Patrick's, Dublin, on view for over two hundred years, has been copied for any number of critical and historical works on its subject, but Johnston maintains that it has never once been reproduced fully and correctly. More important, the documents for the Swift story are papers that are actually in existence and that anyone can study. Yet Johnston found that any careful examination of this source material disclosed that it was "a mass of contradictions, misdescriptions and deliberate mendacity."[4] Further, Swift himself seems to have been responsible for a good deal of this. The upshot is that the mistakes, deliberate and otherwise, in the original documents, plus the errors of carelessness and omission in subsequent scholarship, make it almost impossible to compose anything like a logical and coherent portrait of Swift and his two ladies.

II   *Stella and Vanessa*

Since *The Dreaming Dust* depends rather heavily on some knowledge of Swift for its narrative content, it seems well to sketch briefly the facts of his life as they are generally accepted. The play's chief concern is with Swift's private life, not his public life; with the man and not with his writings. Any discussion therefore must assume an awareness of this material in order to appreciate Johnston's reinterpretation of it.

Swift's father died just before his birth in Dublin in 1667; his uncle, Godwin Swift, was supposedly responsible for his education in Ireland until around 1689 when Jonathan went to England where he became secretary to Sir William Temple who has been variously described as a distant relative (through his wife) of the Swift family or merely a man whose father had been a friend of the Swifts. At Sir William Temple's home, Moor Park in Surrey, Swift became acquainted in 1689 with Bridget Johnson, a servant of Sir William's sister. Mrs. Johnson had three young children, one of whom was Esther (Stella), born 1681. It was common report at the time that Sir William was not only the father of Stella but also that Swift was his illegitimate offspring. After standing for an M.A. at Oxford, Swift returned to Moor Park where he remained until the death of his patron in 1699, except for two and one-half years when he took holy orders and held a vicar's post in northern Ireland. The fact that Esther Johnson seemed to enjoy the special attention of Sir William encouraged the rumors about her parentage; the fact that Swift was her tutor did not cause the rumors to subside.

After Temple's death, Swift returned to Ireland as clergyman in 1700 for a second time; Stella, now twenty, followed him in the company of a distant Temple relation, Mrs. Rebecca Dingley. It is even possible that Sir William may, on his death, have entrusted Stella to Swift (she would have been his only remaining child), and this was why he seemed to stand *in loco parentis,* a fact that Stella's suitors took for granted. Although Temple left her some money, it seems it was not enough. She knew she was partly supported by Swift. Around 1704, one of her suitors, the Reverend William Tisdall, broached the subject of marriage. An understanding seems to have been reached between Swift and Stella at this time with the result that she rejected Tisdall and continued in the same close relationship with Swift for the rest of her life, a curious position with which she seemed content.

Within the next few years on one of his trips to London, probably around 1709–10, Swift made the acquaintance of a widow,
Mrs. Vanhomrigh, whose daughter Esther (Vanessa), born 1688,
evidently fascinated him, and he fascinated her. Swift soon assumed
an informal teacher-student relationship with the young woman.
He had been made Dean of St. Patrick's in Dublin in 1713, and
when the Tory government fell the next year with the death of
Queen Anne, he was forced to return to Ireland to live. Mrs. Vanhomrigh died around the same time, and when Swift departed for
Ireland, Vanessa and her sister also went there to live on some family property at Celbridge. From the latter part of that year until
Vanessa's death nine years later, Swift was "in the equivocal position of having both his women friends of indeterminate status,
living within a few miles of each other and of his Cathedral — a
state of affairs that he clearly did not enjoy, although any distress
in the situation did not result in his crossing either of them off his
visiting list."[5] Despite their proximity, there seems no evidence that
these two ladies ever met, and few people who knew one seemed to
know the other.

How could it last so long, and how could the two women accept
it? Of course, there was the story that Stella didn't accept it and
that sometime during that period she was secretly married to the
Dean, a position Longford adopts in *Yahoo*. The other lady, however, tired of waiting nine years for either a proposal or an explanation, took things into her own hands and wrote Stella, inquiring if
she was Swift's wife. The only response was to have the Dean
return her letter without any explanation, as the story goes, at
which point she tore up her will, chose new executors, and drafted
instructions that allowed them to publish her papers, thus making it
possible to bring her relationship with the famous Dean of St.
Patrick's into the open at some future date. Then she died, leaving
a curious reputation behind her as a foolish young woman who
should have known better than to attach herself to a respectable,
though secretly married, churchman. As Johnston says, "It is
Vanessa who always has to pay, to keep Swift right with the
world."[6]

Meanwhile, Swift and Stella were careful to make it plain that
they did not live as man and wife and were never to be found alone
together, a state of affairs that prevailed until her death. In the
autumn of 1727, Stella became very ill when Swift was in London.
Before hastening back, he wrote a curious letter expressing anxiety

that she not die *"in domo decani"* (in the deanery) where she and Dingley had been staying, evidently fearing her death there would lend substance to the stories that they were man and wife. She lingered until January, 1728, and was buried in Swift's own cathedral. Despite any rumors to the contrary, he did not leave instructions to be buried beside her.

III   *The Search for Swift*

These are the facts of the Swift story as they are usually accepted. But on close inspection, they leave a number of questions unanswered. First, were Swift and Stella ever married? If so, why was the marriage a secret? More to the point, why was it *kept* a secret? If they were not man and wife, why did she not accept another suitor like the Reverend Tisdall? Why did she tolerate a situation in which the world was left to assume she might be Swift's mistress? Why did Swift not marry Vanessa or someone else? Why did his relationship with Vanessa continue so long, only to be broken off suddenly in the spring of 1723? These are the main questions Johnston answers in his portrait of Swift in *The Dreaming Dust* and later in scholarly detail in *In Search of Swift*. There are other questions also which are only slightly less relevant to the play, such as the identity of Swift's true father who could not, as Johnston shows, have been Jonathan Swift the Elder. Why did Swift enshroud details of his life in mystery (e.g., his place of birth)? Why his strange antagonism for Godwin Swift, the uncle who is credited with educating him?

In Search of Swift is a well-documented and convincing study. Johnston maintains that his is the only resolution, using available evidence, to the Swift-Stella-Vanessa problem of why these three behaved as they did. His answers can be summed up briefly; with some additions they are the answers dramatized in *The Dreaming Dust*. Swift was a perfectly normal man who would have wanted to marry Stella, but he knew they were blood relations. However, they were not both the illegitimate children of Sir William Temple, as had been rumored; only Stella was. Swift was the result of an autumnal affair of Sir John Temple, Sir William's father. Jonathan Swift the Elder could not have been the father of the Dean because it can be proved that he died before his son could have been conceived.

Swift the younger was then the half-brother of Sir William, and his relationship with Stella was that of uncle and niece. A marriage between two such relations would not only have been an offense against canon law but also a crime. Swift was fearful that some of his political enemies, of which there were several, would, in the event of his marriage, discover the relationship and use it to disgrace him or even put him in prison. At some point after she became emotionally involved with the Dean, Stella was told or found out the truth of her paternity, perhaps in the crisis precipitated by the Reverend Tisdall's proposal. At that time she decided not to marry Tisdall or, probably, any other man since that would have meant a separation from Swift. She was willing to let people guess about her relationship, and if they only *guessed* she and the Dean were married, nothing could come of it legally. Swift apparently felt he could be faithful in a relationship that was not binding by law.

But in London Swift came into the orbit of Mis Vanhomrigh whom he could love and with whom there would be no bar to physical consummation. Johnston thinks Vanessa probably became Swift's mistress there. But when she expected him to marry her, Vanessa was disappointed; her hopes were crushed when she involved Stella by writing her, for then the Dean broke with her once and for all. Johnston's explanation is logical: Stella imposed on the Dean the condition that if he married Vanessa, he must explain their relationship to the world, lest it be assumed she was a cast-off mistress. This condition Swift finally concluded he neither could nor would meet. It was such matters of his parentage that Swift was trying to conceal when he was vague and contradictory about certain dates and facts. The strange antagonism toward his Uncle Godwin, who supposedly educated him but who could not even properly educate his own sons, may now be explained: the money for Swift's education, which was one of the best to be had, came from Sir John Temple via his son, William, just as Sir William took care to educate his own illegitimate daughter by employing Swift as her tutor. The Temples, it seems, were careful not only to cover their moral lapses but to accept the ensuing responsibilities.

IV   *Seven Sins in a Setting*

The Dean's relationship with the two women in his life is the very fabric of *The Dreaming Dust,* but it is not the theme. As Johnston wrote in his introduction to the play, *Dust* has "long since ceased to be as much concerned with the personal problems of Swift, as with the seven deadly sins, their relative deadliness, and the curious phenomenon that it is usually our own particular sin that we find really unbearable in other people."[7] The result is "an audacious attempt to combine techniques in the Pirandellian and Morality Play modes."[8] *Dust* centers on a group of actors who have been performing "The Masque of the Seven Deadly Sins" in Swift's own cathedral, St. Patrick's, Dublin. The actors are never given names except for the vices they represent. Each one is given an opportunity to explain Swift in terms of the vice he is portraying in the masque, i.e., in terms of his own special weakness which is the shortcoming he finds most objectionable in others. Thus, Johnston universalizes the theme and at the same time anchors it in the particular.

The play is set in 1835; it was in this year that reconstruction caused a portion of the cathedral floor to be opened. Several coffins were exposed to view, and one of them bore Swift's nameplate. The British Association as well as a group of phrenologists were meeting in Dublin, and between their presence and that of curious outsiders, much excitement was generated. Finally two coffins were opened, the one bearing Swift's name and the other beside it which possibly contained the bones of Stella. The sexton, one Macguire, reportedly had it from Swift's servant, Brennan, that Stella's coffin was near the Dean's. The bones were, as Johnston said, "enthusiastically disturbed, dried, measured and passed around Dublin." One portion of Swift's remains was reportedly stolen and taken to the United States. Eventually the bones were returned to Macguire who took it upon himself to put both skulls into the same coffin before resealing it.

The floor was taken up once more in 1882; again the coffin was opened and the two skulls taken out and examined. When they were replaced, concrete was poured over the coffin and the plaque for Swift placed in the floor of the cathedral by the "first distinct pillar." A brass plaque for Stella was placed nearby to indicate that Swift and his lady were together. It was moved several feet away from Swift's in 1924 and moved back again by a new dean in 1935. The background of the 1835 disinterment is necessary to understand the arguments the Seven Deadly Sins are having when the play opens with two women returning the skulls that have been passed around among visiting delegates and other interested Dubliners. However, this background is merely a framework on which to hang the scenes that ultimately reveal complex human relationships.

After the basic situation is established (the setting and the just-concluded performance of the morality play), the Dean of St. Patrick's appears as the two skulls are being examined by the actors and the positions of the graves debated with the sexton, who presumably is Macguire. Swift's successor explains to the group that man is "the inheritor of seven of the most mysterious gifts of the spirit, his sins," one of which will in the end cause his death. He reminds them that until they know which of the seven killed Swift, they cannot solve the riddle of his life, death, and burial. The Dean then requests that the players act as interpreters for the dust of Swift and Stella to determine which of the seven sins shaped their fate; then a decision can be reached as to whether or not they should be in the same grave. "The past is closer than we think," he tells them. "Lend it your lips, my friends, and let it dream aloud."[9]

After the prologue, there are ten scenes of varying length and importance which tell in sometimes confusing, non-chronological order the story of Swift, Vanessa, and Stella. Each of the seven sins is given a brief chance to state his point of view before the scene that emphasizes his speciality, although not in every case is there a strong connection between the sin and the action. Pride and Envy receive the most attention. The structure seems simple enough, but it is worked out with great subtlety; it is finally the story of Swift, not the theme, that dominates the play, thus making the group of actors and the Dean (who always takes the part of Swift) not particularly interesting in their own right. This, however, is merely a vestige of the morality play, for the characters are given neither names nor personalities beyond the sins they represent. Perhaps the simplest way to show Johnston's construction is by means of a table depicting the approximate date of the action, the setting, and Swift's age according to the morality figure controlling the scene:

Sin	Approximate date of action	Setting	Approximate age of Swift
1. Gluttony	late 1730s or early 1740s	The Deanery, Dublin	early 70s
2. Avarice	probably 1709	Laracor, County Meath	early 40s
3. Lust	around 1709–10	Drawing Room, London	early 40s

3a. "	around 1713–14	London	mid-40s
4. Anger	1723	Celbridge	56
5. Envy	1723	The Deanery	56
5a. "	1707–09	Laracor	early 40s
6. Pride	1723	The Deanery	56
6a. "	1723	Celbridge	56
6b. "	1724–27	The Deanery	56–60
7. Sloth	early 1740s	The Deanery	early 70s

V   Gluttony, Avarice, and Lust

In introducing the first of these tableaux, Gluttony charges that Swift was a "vicious pander to his own degraded appetites . . . a dirty, vulgar fellow." The following scene that dramatizes this is relatively tame. The Reverend Tisdall, Stella's disappointed suitor of many years before, calls on the Dean. They are interrupted by a visit from Swift's former cook, now a trollop married to a ballad singer. After begging money of the Dean, the husband sings a satirical ballad about him, causing him to fly into a rage and send them away. Swift quarrels with Tisdall who tells him his work stinks, that he stinks too. "We all stink, Tisdall," Swift replies. "It is the fate of the race of man to stink" (25). There is in this scene the stench of human mortality common to age and decrepitude but not much that suggests gluttony. It is one of the less interesting episodes and one of the less organic in its relation of Swift's character to Johnston's theme.

The Reverend Tisdall, as Avarice points out in the introduction to the following episode, had good reason to feel resentful toward Swift. Since he was disappointed over Stella, his view is naturally biased. For Avarice, it is much simpler: Swift was simply "avaricious in money matters, and in the end this lost for both of them the happiness that they deserved" (26). This scene occurs during the second of those two periods when Swift was a country vicar in northern Ireland. It is one of the stronger scenes, for it depicts the events that led, Johnston thinks, to the reasons Swift gave Stella for not being able to marry her. Here Tisdall proposes to marry Stella; Swift, as her guardian, rejects him. Stella questions Swift's authority over her, and it all leads to the more important question of why he does not marry her himself. Avarice has already explained what he will say, that he cannot support a wife. Stella thinks he is reluctant because she is Sir William Temple's illegitimate daughter, and as a churchman he does not want to marry a bastard. This conversation between Swift and Stella will be resumed in another scene, and Avarice concludes that whatever may have been spoken in their interview, "she came back from the orchard with a smile on her calm, proud face, and never mentioned marriage again" (32). In any case, "...money must have been at the back of it."

The Lust episode is in two scenes; appropriately the setting is now London where Swift encounters the Widow Vanhomrigh and Vanessa. In the first scene, Vanessa is an adept flirt and verbal fencer of the sort who might capture the imagination of a man in his early forties (she was twenty years his junior). The scene ends with the fall of the Whigs from power and the formation of a government by Robert Harley in whose administration Swift played a major role as one of the most powerful men in England, thanks to his willingness to put his abilities as a political pamphleteer at the service of the Tories. Lust's second scene demonstrates the length of Swift's involvement with Vanessa: first, he has written for her the still charming "Cadenus and Vanessa" ("Cadenus" is an anagram for "Decanus," the Dean); second, Charles Ford, a close friend of Swift who seems to have been the only man who knew both women well, warns him that Vanessa expects him to marry her. As the Dean grows angry at this, a bell tolls the death of Queen Anne and the fall of the Tories that will send Swift back to Ireland in what would be virtually exile and where Vanessa will follow him. For Lust, it is all simple: Swift's besetting sin was "a lusty one that might be forgiven in you or me, but was fatal in a man of God."

VI   *Anger, Envy, and Pride*

Episode four moves ahead a whole decade to the last days of Swift's and Vanessa's friendship. The scene is properly chosen to demonstrate Anger's contention that Swift was a "bully and a tormentor" who was ruled by "anger and resentment against a world he loathed, and a sex he was determined to humiliate" (42). It profiles an anxious woman who has waited a long time and a man who is a political exile; it is even briefly a love story but one that quickly erupts in anger, terminating with Vanessa's demand to know the truth of Swift's relationship with Stella. His answer is simple, too simple. He throws her own crumpled letter at her feet. But mere anger is no explanation, and so this scene must be continued later by another of the seven sins who views the outcome in a different way.

The Envy episode is in two sections with an interlude. It is the key scene of the play in terms of explaining the relationship between Swift and Stella. The first half, which is the less effective, is designed to demonstrate that Swift was "not a big man at all" but quite petty and jealous of anyone more successful than himself. The immediate object of his jealousy is Dr. Berkeley, later Bishop of Cloyne; their altercation is dramatized briefly before being interrupted by annoyed actors. Swift comments to the other churchman that when he was chaplain to the Lord Lieutenant, he was so poor he was obliged to keep a coffee house. In what seems an attempt to impress, Berkeley responds by alluding to a duke's offer of a chaplaincy which he rejected. Swift counters with a reference to his political power in Ireland. As Vanessa's letter to Stella arrives from Celbridge, Berkeley explains that he would not accept the patronage of a bastard (the duke): " 'What if his father was a king, . . . his mother was a harlot.' " All of this is more subtle than simply verbal fencing between two proud men. The words "bastard" and "harlot" cut deeply here for both Swift and Stella, not only foreshadowing the pivotal issue between them of their blood relationship but also providing a bridge to the rest of the scene that follows the actors' interruption.

At this point, the actors break in, complaining that the rest of the scene "makes no sense." It is, of course, Stella's reaction to Vanessa's letter that the players do not understand. The actress playing both Pride and Stella complains her role is not believable, now that she knows so much about Swift's relationship with Vanessa. To stand by and say nothing makes the woman a kind of nonentity. If Swift has a reason for what he is doing, it is one he is too proud to admit, she insists, "But what about my pride?" The full explanation, of course, came after the conclusion of the second episode (Avarice), and so the setting now changes to Laracor to play out that answer, given in the orchard, which so satisfied Stella that she reappeared smiling and never mentioned the matter again.

The clock is turned back approximately fourteen years, and Swift is again in his early forties as he walks with Stella in the orchard after Tisdall's proposal. Here it is clear she knows Sir William Temple is her father. The ugly, disturbing word that Berkeley had employed by chance is the answer, she thinks, to the Dean's failure to marry her: "The vicar of Laracor could never condescend to marry a bastard." Here Swift explains Johnston's theory of both their births; both being illegitimate offspring of father and son respectively, their blood relationship is so close that marriage would not only be a crime against Church and State but also incestuous. Stella then agrees to marry Tisdall, but Swift reminds her they could not see each other. She realizes he would prefer her not to marry at all, to stay single and simply remain his friend. He does not foresee that some day he would need a kind of love she cannot give: "I am Jonathan Swift, and I want nothing from any human being that I cannot get from you" (60).

As the scene with Dr. Berkeley is resumed ("...you were saying something about somebody's mother being a harlot"), Pride presents her view of Swift. The dean has learned that Vanessa ignored his warning and brought Stella into their relationship by writing to her, demanding to know if she is his wife. This produces Swift's major dilemma in the play. To explain to Vanessa that he is not married would lead her to expect a proposal. Yet marriage to her (and the idea seems to appeal to him) would force him to leave Stella who could not or would not stay near him, just as her marriage to the Reverend Tisdall would have separated them at his own insistence. To marry Vanessa without any public explanation would humiliate Stella. Therefore, she is right to impose one condition on his marriage to Vanessa: to tell the world the truth of what lies between them. This is a condition he cannot accept, even though it dooms him to a life of celibacy. When the Dean returns Vanessa's letter to her, he does so without speaking to her; there is no explanation he can give. He wronged her, Johnston believes, through his inability to be cruel. "When cruelty was the only thing that could have saved her, he should have been cruel." He wronged her through "the demonic pity that was the keystone of his character."[10]

By means of a spotlight, the scene changes to Swift who is kneeling in prayer while the ghostly voice of Stella accuses him of pride, "the sin that cannot bring itself to pray for pardon, ... the most deadly of the seven." This transitional interlude leads to Pride's third scene — a scene without much cohesion, for it tries to do too much — in which Charles Ford reminds Swift that the publication of "Cadenus and Vanessa" has made him the object of gossip. When Berkeley, one of Vanessa's new executors, appears, Ford tells him that the publication of the lady's papers is causing Stella much grief. She is seriously ill, and Berkeley overhears Swift's offer to her to tell the truth of their relationship. But it is too late. As Swift prays that she not die in the Deanery, Berkeley remonstrates with him, and Stella returns to defend the Dean in what is almost a love scene.

VII   *Sloth: Summation and Conclusion*

The interlude at this point, when the actors drop their roles as the Seven Sins to speak briefly with the sexton, is a kind of summation. The sexton, who has decided to bury the two skulls together, speaks for Johnston when he sarcastically asks the actors: "What do any of youse know about his sins, except maybe the one that happens to be your own? That's the only one that nobody can forgive" (71). Lust agrees that each has accused the Dean of his own particular weakness, for it is "the only sin that any of us can understand." Even Stella? asks Pride. Stella most of all, replies Lust, for she used to say that Swift would not be outdone in anything, but in her pride she outdid even him. That is why they should lie in the same tomb: "They were of the same blood in more ways than one."

Sloth, the last of the Seven Sins, is shortchanged. In the last minutes of the play, there is a brief scene in which he appears as Swift's servant, Brennan. Swift is old and ill and only a few years from death. As Dingley reads from the Book of Job, the Dean gives her instead some stanzas of his own, "On the Death of Dr. Swift." As Brennan brings in a crowd of Dublin rabble, charging them sixpence to "have a look at the mad Dean," Swift rises from his chair with the words, "I am that I am" and accuses them all of being Yahoos. After flinging a Bible at them, he repeats his words, and the choir is heard offstage chanting a portion of the service. As they file out of the cathedral, the play ends.

Swift's words in this scene (which, as noted earlier, Lord Longford had also employed in *Yahoo*) are from Shakespeare's Sonnet CXXI (" 'Tis better to be vile than vile esteemed"): ". . . I am that I am, and they that level / At my abuses reckon up their own. . . ."

Swift's words here are not only a reference to his detractors during his lifetime but also a subtle reminder of Johnston's theme. In one sense, Johnston's portrait of Swift is an answer to those who have tried to encompass this complex man in a single view. The playwright attempts to account logically for Swift's behavior, avoiding, however, a facile summing up that would never resolve the complexities of such a mass of contradictions. If Johnston's Swift is a victim of hubris, his pride is so balanced with pity that the one cancels out the other. What remains is a man very like, but greater than, other men, composed in slightly unequal parts of seven weaknesses. *The Dreaming Dust* is a fascinating portrait that moves beyond the strictures of biography to make a wise and compassionate comment about all men.

CHAPTER 7

Johnston's Inferno: Nine Rivers from Jordan *and* A Fourth for Bridge

I *A Playwright's New Role*

IN 1936 Johnston gave up his profession of barrister to join the British Broadcasting Corporation (BBC) in London; by the following year, he was actively involved with television production. His work with the American Liaison Unit for the BBC in 1939–40 and his experience as reporter in both Ireland and England made him a logical choice to cover World War II, despite the fact that he had never seen action, something he shared with most of his fellow correspondents. Accordingly, in July, 1942, he arrived in Cairo determined to avoid propaganda and, in words echoing the court-room oath, "to describe soberly and sensibly exactly what I saw, and give the people at home the truth, the whole truth, and nothing but the truth, whether happy or unfavorable."[1] It did not take long to discover that the pitfalls of this simplistic if admirable creed lay in the peculiar ambiguity of battlefield truth, but out of the experiences of these years (he served until the end of the war) came *Nine Rivers from Jordan.* This work was based, as he tells in a Preface that appears in the last third of the book, on "a collection of diaries, personal papers, radio scripts, *graphitae* and pamphlets that were annotated, elaborated and finally put into some sort of shape ... in ... 1947" (333).

The book, which appeared first in England in 1953 and (minus a final section) in America in 1955, is a fascinating volume difficult to classify since it goes far beyond the usual World War II memoir. It is worth careful consideration for at least four reasons: first and most important, it is an extraordinary spiritual autobiography with mythic overtones; it also has, in the narrator-acolyte, one of the most complex versions of the Johnston hero; it contains the germ of Johnston's only one-act play, *A Fourth for Bridge;* and it is the source of an unusually complex libretto which Johnston himself wrote for an opera of the same name with music by Hugo Weisgall.

II   *The Quest*

On its most elementary level, *Nine Rivers from Jordan* is a war memoir, the autobiography of a war correspondent during the years 1942–45; on this level alone it is a compelling story. Johnston arrived in Africa in time to report the Battle of El Alamein and followed the Allied sweep through Italy, France, Belgium, and into Germany for the final days of the war. But this is not simply a historical account; the correspondent, who is Johnston's persona, is after bigger game than "the whole truth." He confesses to feeling a little guilty in not trying to write a historical account, but there are others who will do that. There are not many, however, "who will put on paper what it was really like." The real intention of *Nine Rivers* is not "to represent the experience of any particular man, but of a concourse and of a generation," for on its most complex level, the book is a spiritual autobiography centering around a symbolic journey or quest which is valid not only for the narrator (Johnston's name never occurs except on the title page) but for all men at mid-century. In this respect, it is closer to the dramatist's early play, *A Bride for the Unicorn,* than to anything else he has written.

The quest is initiated on a purely narrative level with an episode (which may or may not have actually happened, he tells us later) following shortly on his arrival in Egypt. In the moonlight at the base of the giant pyramid, a dragoman reads the correspondent's palm and tells him that before long he will begin a journey "over earth, over fire, over air, and over water." The dragoman cannot tell where this journey will lead but only that he will go "from where it is white to where it will be white again . . . from a depth to a summit." He also sees that there are nine rivers to be crossed, and at the end there is "something that I do not understand, something about a dove" (34–5). When the correspondent has reached the last river, he will find what he has been looking for. This motif of the quest/journey is developed on many levels of realism, symbolism, and myth: the new correspondent's search for the elusive "front lines" in the desert war where he may be baptized as an on-the-spot reporter; his search for a German girl named Anneliese Wendler, the "third Eve" to whom the book is dedicated; the search of an Odysseus for Ithaca and Penelope; the search of a Job for answers to the "Why?" of God's torments; the search of a Faust for love; the search of an Adam to understand the God who tempts with forbidden fruit; finally and most significantly, the search of Man to understand himself, his world, and his God in terms of that God's bequest of both Good and Evil. This wartime odyssey is a journey that seems to "parallel the course of life itself, from childhood to maturity — a journey, maybe, in search of its own meaning" (349).

III   *The Triadic Structure*

Nine Rivers is divided into three nearly equal parts, the first and shortest of which, "The Catechumens," covers approximately seven months of the war in Africa. The title here is undoubtedly meant to suggest both the war correspondent as neophyte and the man as a moral novice under instruction, particularly as he learns (1) the difference between the "myth of our motives and the truth of our intentions, between what we imagine we are doing and what really happens" (127); and (2) the elusive nature of truth, for nobody, certainly not the military, "is in a position to place a finger unerringly on the points that really matter, and say, This is the truth about the situation" (128). Part II, "The Faithful," covers the last quarter of 1943 to mid-1944, the months in Italy — Anzio, Cassino, Rome, Perugia, Naples, Assisi — and two brief forays into the Balkans. The title presumably refers to the now-seasoned reporter doing his job as well as to the man who, having experienced a time of skepticism, arrives at a plateau of qualified faith. Part III, "The Epiklesis," covers the months from the autumn of 1944 to the late spring of 1945. This section embodies a natural climax and conclusion for the whole book as it moves not only toward the end of the war but also toward a satisfying accommodation on the part of the narrator with certain spiritual and moral issues.

IV   *The Nine Crossings*

Nine Rivers has an extremely loose, picaresque "plot," but structurally it is quite strong because it is built around the "crossings" of the nine rivers of the title. These "crossings" serve both as markers of geographical progress on the correspondent's journey through the battle zones and as stages in the narrator's changing attitudes about such matters as the war itself, the nature of his assignment, his own involvement as a neutral, the various national and racial groups he encounters, the postwar plans for the conquered, and finally larger issues like death, guilt, innocence, evil, and God whom the narrator dubs "Old Nobodaddy."

The author also adopts the device of naming the rivers after the nine Greek muses, each of whom might be thought of as offering appropriate inspiration for a particular stage of the journey. The first river is the Jordan, the River of Polymnia, muse of song, where the narrator is symbolically baptized as he "anoints" his sweaty forehead for relief from heat and dust. The Nile he associates with Terpsichore, the muse of dance. As in some other cases, the association here seems a rather arbitrary one. The third river, the Sangro in Italy, is assigned to Euterpe, the muse of lyric poetry. The Tiber, the fourth river, is presided over by Clio, the muse of history, one of the more obvious pairings. The fifth river, the Seine, is slyly named after Erato, the muse of love poetry. The narrative depicts a comic search for that fabled brothel that is always in another city and of another time, but never at hand. The river of Thalia, the comic muse, is the storyteller's affectionate nod to the River Liffey in his own native Ireland where he returns briefly during the war to take a wife. The Rhine is the seventh, appropriately named the River of Melpomene after the muse of tragedy, as the Wehrmacht retreats into its homeland in the early months of 1945. The river of Calliope, muse of epic poetry, is the Danube, where the correspondent spent some time during the last days of the war. The Inn is the last river, named for Urania, the muse of astronomy; the relationship here between river and muse may suggest a burst of light after a period of darkness: "Turn on the stars! Turn on the moon and the sun, for we have crossed the Inn, and are going up the Brenner."

The last scene of the book takes place in the Brenner Pass; this is the "height" of the dragoman's prophecy. The narrator has gone from where it is white (the "ivory desert" and the "snow-white dunes" of sand of the early chapters) to where it will be white again (the snows of the Austrian Alps). But what of the "dove" the dragoman could not understand? On the Italian side of the

Brenner, there is a stone memorial dating from World War I. On it is engraved the fragment: "Sia sacra agli Italiani la via dove passarono i fanti" ("Whether the road where the infantrymen would pass is sacred to Italians"). Here is the "dove" which in Italian means "where," the place where he will find what he has been looking for.

V   *Levels of Meaning*

In a somewhat different preface to Part III in the English edition, Johnston calls attention to "the varying levels of analogue in the text": for example, the biological structure, which begins with birth in "this wrinkled vulva of the world" (the valley of the Dead Sea) and moves through the baptism in the Jordan to the snows of senility in the wintry Brenner Pass; the "liturgical format" initiated with the "Introit" and concluding with the "Ite Missa Est"; the "temporal span," a long night of wars beginning at sunset in Egypt and concluding with the end of hostilities at sunrise in the Austrian Alps; and the "dialectical parallelism," moving from Homer through Blake and Goethe and back to the Book of Job.[2] *Nine Rivers* is reminiscent of *The Old Lady Says "No!"* in the network of allusions that operates throughout. In its multi-level presentation of a "progress," it recalls the complexity of *A Bride for the Unicorn.*

VI   *The Narrator as Reporter*

It is rewarding to approach *Nine Rivers* first of all simply on the level of reportage. Generally, the reporter keeps the rest of the man in the background. That Johnston's name is never used throughout the book is not merely an oversight but is "in simple averment of the fact that the name is of no importance." The reader never really gets to know much of the reporter's private life during these years beyond his role in the war; one learns nothing, for example, of the successful dramatist. One knows only that the writer is separated from his wife, that a divorce has for some time been pending, and that he regrets being unable to play the role of father to his son.

The narrator as war correspondent, however, is a somewhat more complicated person. He presents himself to the reader as a beginner who, despite his experience with the BBC and his work for the stage, has admittedly much to learn in a different kind of theater. In addition, *what* he learns in the course of covering the war leads him to increasingly complex moral questions about the evil that has brought on the holocaust, questions that are really the primary philosophic concerns of the book. At first, the correspondent is happily uncomplicated in his aim to report the war objectively and factually. Eventually he realizes there are enough facts to prove or disprove anything he might write; thus the reporter, he concludes, must be a cross between a judge and a detective. He becomes progressively more concerned with the problem of human motives, "why" we fight rather than "how." By the time he arrives at the gates of Buchenwald, any reflections on his temporary profession have completely given way to the more urgent matters of the "who" and "why" of the death camp.

The book includes only two or three brief sections that are in the form of broadcast scripts, and despite the correspondent's averment that he is not a "literary gent," his reports for the BBC must have been highly effective if his style in these is any indication. His report of a night air raid over Libya, the sweep on Tobruk, a brief trip to the Balkans, a visit to the Anzio beachhead, a mine-laying air raid over the Danube, an audience with Pope Pius XII after the occupation of Rome by the Allies, the searing revelations of Buchenwald — all represent reporting of a high order that goes beyond the essential facts and conveys the tension and excitement of a situation by capturing its very essence. The author, one might submit, can do this better than most simply because he *is* a "literary gent" and brings a genuine writer's imagination to the subject.

VII   *A Neutral's Position*

Ireland assumed a neutral position in World War II, although it made a significant contribution in fighting men when thousands of the Irish National Volunteers were not just allowed but actually encouraged to enlist in the British Army (where they were known as the National Volunteers). A similar neutrality colored Johnston's personal views from the beginning of his apprenticeship and so is reflected in the attitudes of his correspondent-persona. One reviewer came close to the truth when he labelled the author a "benevolent neutral"[3]; to another reviewer Johnston was "an Irish will-o-the-wisp who happened in on the holocaust not caring — at first — who won."[4] Of course, this neutrality is evident in his stance as the objective observer who purports to deal only in facts. It can be seen in his interest (perhaps more understandable now than then) in reporting the "good" of *both* sides: e.g., an account of a German officer who carried a wounded Britisher into Allied lines and explained his action by saying, "...if I had done nothing he would have died." CBS correspondent Winston Burdett insisted that one could not take a "gentlemanly view" of the war because the Nazis were so ruthless. But if some of *them* are gentlemen, is there anything wrong in saying so, wonders the narrator. Only a few days after the dragoman's prophecy, he is beginning to question what the war is about, a problem that continues to plague him almost until the end of the book.

VIII   *The Jordan*

The "crossings" of the rivers that mark the stages of moral and spiritual growth begin in the cradle of civilization. Johnston's persona refers to these months as his Homeric period: "The milestones of this journey are like the footsteps of the race. In some odd and rather mystical way they seem to parallel the course of life itself, from childhood to maturity..." (349). The Palestine Campaign brings him from Egypt to Jerusalem and from there to Azrak for a dinner with the Arab Legion. This episode is a turning point, like "the start of a pilgrimage, or the source of a river." At the Jordan, the first of the nine, he recalls the words of the prophecy: "from a depth to a summit"; there is, he observes, "no depth deeper than this one, and if I am destined to cross nine rivers, what better start can I make than with Jordan?" (71) Intuitively, he senses that he shall travel in safety so long as he goes unarmed. "I am not in this war as a belligerent, and so long as I remain in my own role and refrain from carrying arms, the war can do me no harm" (72). This seems to be the message spoken by a voice out of "this wrinkled vulva of the world," the valley of the Dead Sea, and he decides to act accordingly.

Unlike many believers, the correspondent is not disillusioned by his first visit to modern Jerusalem. However, he finds it "hard to follow the Christian all the way to Calvary, if indeed Calvary exists at all" (74). After an argument with a fellow correspondent who is a self-proclaimed atheist and refuses to enter the Holy Sepulchre, the narrator concludes that the man is accepting the truth of the Christian argument as he defines it and is railing against it, whereas he himself would merely contradict its truth. The "atheist" did not disbelieve at all. "In fact, if anybody is the unbeliever it must be me, for I do not take such a gloomy or such an orthodox view of creation" (77). Yet, he finds no particular feeling of evil in himself. This is the catechumen speaking; the voices of God and the muses have posed no questions and given no answers as yet.

IX   *The Nile*

The "crossing" of the Nile is chiefly a preface to more significant issues. It does, however, introduce a romantic motif into the search. In an abandoned German vehicle, the reporter finds a bundle of letters and photographs, the documents of a brief romance that had begun in Eckartsberga, a small village in Thuringia, where a soldier-lover named George Sicherman had been stationed. The girl's name is Anneliese Wendler, and she functions on an elementary level as one objective of the search: the narrator's attempt to return her love letters. Initially, she merely symbolizes the temptation to pity; later she evokes Marguerite in the correspondent's *Faust*-fantasy; finally and most significantly, she is the "Pietà," the Mater Dolorosa, the Mother of God and mankind, and the eternal victim of the world's injustice. But at first, Anneliese is simply an ordinary, moderately attractive German girl who works in a local *gasthaus* and who wishes to continue the romance with George Sicherman. The discovery of her letters is immediately followed by the war correspondent's first face-to-face encounter with the enemy, a German soldier, who, after Rommel's retreat, wanted to surrender to him personally. The man is "no baffled aggressor" who is faced with the consequences of his evil deeds. On the contrary, their conversation, until the captive is turned over to someone in authority, is pleasant and informative enough. If this is not exactly the narrator's first temptation to pity, it is certainly the kind of evidence that causes him greatly to underestimate Nazi Germany's culpability. Later, after the capture of Tobruk, he returns to the subject of the letters of Anneliese Wendler. Her invitation to the soldier to return to her village of Eckartsberga prompts the reporter to wonder if that is where he is going, where he will find the dove on the summit. The answer — much later — is affirmative, for Anneliese's letters lead to a gateway with the legend, *"Recht oder Unrecht — Mein Vaterland."*

The correspondent's Homeric first section concludes with a slightly cynical admission of the difference between motive and truth, "between what we imagine we are doing and what really happens.'' He strongly insists that ''men on the whole are sane,'' and, surprisingly, that war is not really such an evil thing. ''How can it be evil if, in it, one lives more abundantly, and experiences a deeper sense of the meaning of life?'' (136). It need not be ''some sordid squabble'' but, like a game, may be played ''according to certain fixed principles and assumptions.'' Admitting that this is a heretical statement, the author nevertheless concludes that inasmuch as war is inevitable, ''it is more important to keep it the good thing that it is, than to win or to lose it'' (136). By the end of the Homeric period, the quest has not advanced very far; the catechumen's moral sense is still naive and idealistic after two ''crossings.''

X   *The Sangro and the Tiber*

The second section of *Nine Rivers,* ''The Faithful,'' involves only two ''crossings,'' but philosophically it is more interesting than what has gone before; there are more questions of a significant nature, a few answers, and a perceptible change from catechumen to keeper of the faith, however qualified that faith may be. En route to Italy to report the Italian Campaign, the narrator reads *Mein Kampf* and only then begins to realize the scope of the tragedy. It is not Hitler's genius as a leader that produced the holocaust but simply coincidence and ''our own bloody slackness.'' His belief that the war is largely the result of mankind's carelessness leads to a fuller development of the problem signified by the ''crossings'' of the third and fourth rivers, the Sangro and the Tiber.

Early in this section, the narrator is still a catechumen, but shortly after arriving in Italy, he provides the script of an encounter he had with a priest. It is written in the form of a dialogue between Doubtful (the correspondent) and Holy Orders (a priest), facetiously introduced in a style owing much to the Bible and to John Bunyan (''Now it happened within the space of a few days that there journeyed together through these regions...''). The conversation centers around man's choice to fight or not, and on which side. The ''padre'' insists it is not a choice between good and evil; it is just that everybody is cast into roles ''like actors in a play,'' and that is the real tragedy of war. But if there is no good or evil, why fight? How can one justify war at all? The priest's reply is significant for the development of this theme in the rest of the book: ''War is a curse that man brings down upon himself through evil. You don't justify a curse'' (160).

Doubtful then recalls an argument he once heard that it is "all God's malicious doing," which seems reasonable enough if man has to die for nothing at all. If he can be saved only by the miracle of grace, then God is demonic, and good and evil are illusory. The priest responds with the lesson of the Sangro: Hitler is an evil man who makes other men evil. Nothing good can flourish under such a man. Evil is infectious, for like a disease, it breeds. When the war is over, he concludes, and Hitler has been disposed of, we will find ourselves doing everything that he has done and worse. The disease of evil will have spread. Doubtful seems to accept the thesis, for he modifies his earlier position that youth, himself included, regards war as a glamorous diversion. Recalling the days of the Black and Tans in Ireland, the New Zealanders who take few prisoners, and the air raids carried out at random to oblige him and the BBC, he realizes that he has been shaking hands with murderers all his life.

The lesson of the Tiber begins with the narrator's visit to St. Peter's where he finds himself in front of Michelangelo's *Pietà* which reminds him of someone whom he cannot name. Later, he still does not recall where he had seen the face of the figure before, that "second Eve" who had not really freed her children from the sins of the first Eve but had only offered them forgiveness for errors in the work of creation. "But who was going to forgive God?" he wonders. "Would there have to be a third Eve to answer that?" (284). Then the correspondent recalls the photo of a blonde country girl he had almost forgotten. The face of the *Pietà* resembled Anneliese's. This is the last of the "third Eve" — for such she is — for some time, but the image of the wholesome German girl as temptress is important later in resolving the philosophic question of the source of evil.

In the last chapter of this section, the correspondent meets another priest; the incident recalls the earlier encounter with Holy Orders at the Sangro. What can the Church offer me, the reporter inquires. And the priest, speaking for the muse of history, replies: only the accumulated wisdom of the human race. This wisdom would suggest acceptance of the Holy Scriptures, tested as they are by time, but the war correspondent cannot resolve the Gospel of Love with the concept of eternal punishment in Hell. If you take one, replies the priest, you must and can take both, and he gives him a copy of St. Francis' *The Mirror of Perfection*.

At the conclusion of the "crossing" of the Tiber, the narrator has experienced a definite change of attitude, although it cannot be compared to the revelation that comes at Buchenwald sometime later. After reading St. Francis, he realizes that, like many of his generation, he is interested in talking about religion, but the topic is suspect. Why cannot the Church offer a homogeneous faith? Perhaps it is no faith at all if one can divide it in two, believing in one half (Love) and rejecting the other (Hell). The cedar-bound copy of the Bible he bought in Jerusalem offers a resolution as one day he considers the words of Isaiah:

I am the lord, and there is none else.

I form the light, and create darkness: I make peace, and create evil: I the Lord do all these things. (Ch. 45:6–7)

Perhaps it is the Church and not himself that wants only half. If God freely confesses to evil as well as good, then faith is possible, for it is not even necessary to know why He created evil. It is enough to know that faith is not a trap and He is "neither a bungler nor a demon." The problem is left to rest here as the chapter and Part II conclude on a lighter note.

XI *From the Seine to the Liffey*

"The Epiklesis," the last and most important section of the book, covers the Central European phase of the narrator's wartime career. Despite a note of acceptance at the end of Part II, the search continues, and he still does not know exactly what it is he is looking for. The reader is reminded again that the quest and journey are mythic when the correspondent compares the "crossings" to "the course of life itself, from childhood to maturity." With middle age come thoughts concerning religion: it is a point at which the "accumulated wisdom and experience of the human race ceases to be a thing to be contradicted on principle." The fear of the "half" of faith which he rejects (Hell)) is not that important; even so, religion does have a meaning, though what it is he does not know: "I shall take nobody's verdict until I have found out for myself. Maybe that is what I am looking for . . ." (350).

If the second period of the narrator's odyssey was peopled by "the children of Machiavelli," then it is appropriate that on the last phase of his war journey he is conducted by the Americans, the children of the New World. They are not directly responsible, however, for the encounter with Erato, the muse of love poetry, and the "crossing" of the Seine, the fifth river. The visit to Paris comes about through a short stay in the hospital and is, like much of the latter part of the book, simply narration of a high order with several familiar leitmotifs: Irish neutrality coupled with the reporter's own doubts about the war, the problem of evil, the genocide of the Jews, the postwar fate of the Third Reich, the divorce settlement of a first marriage, the separation from his son, and the fear that as the war winds down the Allies will grow ruthless. Even after a visit to a pair of concentration camps near Strasbourg, the correspondent's humanity in touched with pity as he concludes that it is less horrible to endure than to inflict. Half-seriously he wonders what it would be like to change sides in the war.

Thalia, the happy muse of comedy, reigns over the "crossing" of the Liffey. The Johnston-persona manages to get orders that will allow him to return to Dublin briefly to marry a girl who was an actress at the Abbey Theatre (Betty Chancellor, Johnston's present wife). This is a romantic interlude in a story that in some respects owes more to *The Iliad* than to *The Odyssey*.

XII   *Eckartsberga to Buchenwald*

The correspondent returns to Germany and the war where he must confront the old issues; a nonfraternization law irritates him, and he resolves to break it as often as he can. The unlawful looting by the Allies is balanced by the lines of internees and ex-prisoners of war of the Nazis. The sentimental Germany he once knew is difficult to resolve with the country that is now universally despised. Now that Germany is about to pay for her sins, it no longer seems to matter who was responsible for the war. Arriving at Naumburg, he remembers that Eckartsberga, the village of the blonde Anneliese, is not far away. As if he were fulfilling a prophecy, he arrives on schedule, but there are no depths, no summits, and no dove.

Chapters 11, 12, and 13 constitute the resolution of the quest. The first, an account of the liberation of Buchenwald, is the most searing in its impact on the narrator, for here is the evidence that was lacking, the education that will bring him out of his neutrality and conquer the temptation to pity evoked by Anneliese, the "third Eve." As the correspondent recalls the girl, now idealized by his imagination, he remembers lines from her letters, particularly the poignant "I had begun to think that you, unfaithful man, had forgotten Eckartsberga." Once in the village, he is unable to find any trace of her; the civilians say they know nothing, and if they did, they probably would never tell a man in uniform. He cannot even give chocolate to a sullen, hungry youngster who reminds him of his own son; the boy merely runs from him.

Finally an American officer directs him down a road from Eckartsberga where he finds a gate set in barbed-wire fencing. Over it is the legend: *Rechts oder Unrecht — Mein Vaterland* ("My Country Right or Wrong"). And further on over an inner gate: *Jedem das Seinem* ("To Each His Own"). Beyond the gate is the knowledge of the temptress, the knowledge of the reality behind the smiling blonde of the photograph. The narrator does not linger long over a detailed description of the conditions that still prevailed in Buchenwald even after its liberation, nor for that matter does he document at great length the impact it had on him. It is summed up in brief agony that marks the soul forever. He learns that evil infects; he who had chronicled a war, unarmed as was proper, takes a contraband gun, a Luger, as a souvenir. The gun immediately becomes a symbol of the contagion of evil; like the Germans who had lived by it, he is then fated to die by it. Hence, his account of his own death in the last brief moments of the book.

He had laughed at ugly rumors of the death camps and argued with fellow correspondents who had urged a more realistic, less charitable attitude toward the Germans, laughed and argued because he did not want to believe man was capable of such depravity. But what he sees at Buchenwald is "no passing cruelty or wanton act of destruction" but something quite deliberate. "This is the intentional flower of a race theory. This is what logic divorced from conscience can bring men to. This is the wilful dehumanization of the species, and an offence against man himself" (444). Even worse is the fact that good will has been used to betray, and reason employed to hoodwink, indicating that "good will is a mistake — that destruction is our only means of preservation." How could he ever have doubted that there is not an absolute in good and evil, he wonders. This is the horrible end of the search for Anneliese and her George. It was to have come in Eckartsberga, but it is Buchenwald that holds the answer.

XIII   *A* Faust-*play*

The visit to Buchenwald is the real climax, not only of the search but also of the book. However, the narrator has two more "crossings," and before these, there is a chapter quite different from anything else in *Nine Rivers*. It is as though the author, after the bleak confrontation with one of the most infamous spectacles of the twentieth century, must turn in exorcism to some other form to express and come to terms with this new knowledge. He calls this chapter "The High Court on the Brocken," and it takes the form of a fantastic *Faust*-play, with the narrator as Faust and Anneliese in the brief role of Marguerite. The focal point of this parody is the trial scene where Faust, along with "an ex-paperhanger and *agent provocateur* from Central Europe," is tried for misconduct in a public place. Some of the dialogue here is quite amusing, and the cast of characters is simply an amalgam of names of major and minor figures from the entire book.

The trial moves rapidly, and at times Faust hedges and tries frantically to shift onto someone else the blame for the "disorderly conduct" that was World War II. "Blame the dirty little propagandists," he concludes, convicting himself out of his own mouth, for the prosecution observes that he is, ironically, employed as a propagandist. The trial then focuses on the real culprits, the human race, whose governments merely carry out its wishes. After the suggestion that nature should not be held responsible for the failure of *homo sapiens,* the Judge concludes that no sentence of death is necessary since the prisoners have been trying to destroy themselves anyway; they shall be given their hearts' desire, the *"Endwaffe."* This excursion into fantasy is not only welcome relief but also a spiritual inventory of the human race.

XIV   *The Danube and the Inn*

The epic muse, Calliope, is invoked for the "crossing" of the penultimate river. The correspondent, now covering the war along the Danube, carries, in violation of orders and convention, a Luger. He is clearly looking for trouble which comes in various guises, one of which is an Austrian schoolteacher in whose house he and his AP associate are billeted. Some parts of the house have been damaged by casual looting, and the *fraulein* confronts the reporter who admits that perhaps German troops have not behaved that way but reveals to her horror the story of freight cars stacked with starved bodies from the camps. When she asks what this has to do with her, he replies that it has approximately the same to do with her as her pillaged apartment has to do with him, for perhaps both are guilty, but he would still rather be "on my side than on yours."

I have rediscovered a positive belief in right and wrong and am going to cling to it. The trouble with the world of my generation has been that we have thrown out with our lying religion the old belief in a code of moral conduct. And all that we have to put in its place is a logic based on the idea that results are the only thing that matter — a logic that is only tempered by a fear of the big stick. [I.e., what Johnston had called Functionalism in his Preface to *The Golden Cuckoo*]

Buchenwald was the result of that doubt of the existence of an absolute in good and evil. But it does exist, however maliciously successful life may be in confusing us as to which is which. (476)

Good has become a trap, he tells her, and pity a trick. But because some men are evil, must all others be evil too, she asks. The *fraulein* can accept his blaming her or blaming Germany, but she cannot accept his indictment of pity. He replies that there is no other way unless he blames God. "Then," she replies, "you must learn to forgive God." This is the lesson of the Danube.

The conclusion of the narrative comes in Innsbruck as the last river, the Inn, is "crossed," the river of Urania, muse of astronomy. If the dragoman's prophecy holds true, the journey will end in a high place, white like the sands of the Libyan desert, and presided over by the sign of the dove. The end of the war on the Austrian-Italian front is the interesting background for this story: how the surrender of Innsbruck was first tendered to a war correspondent; how the two Allied armies met just over the Brenner Pass on the Italian side; and how the Luger taken at Buchenwald finally led to personal destruction.

The concluding incident is brief. A high-ranking Nazi sits in his car just beyond the Pass in Italy; he is wounded and soon to be a captive. The correspondent joins him; a conversation ensues. As the narrator listens to Otto Suder, the Nazi, he reflects on the whole scheme of war and the senselessness of harsh punishment for the loser. For Suder's benefit, he envisions Germany's punishment after the conflict and the period that came to be known as the Cold War. Suder wonders why the Nazis should be called war criminals if the Allies are going to repeat German atrocities on the defeated. The correspondent explains that it makes no difference what they are called; their defeat is all that will be remembered. Pity will again be a trap to pardon the criminals who will start it all again. Therefore, Suder must die or be allowed to commit suicide. The Luger changes hands as the correspondent offers the Nazi a chance to take his own life, but in a scene worthy of Raymond Chandler, the gun is turned on its owner, and the Nazi presses the trigger.

XV   *After Such Knowledge*

The American edition concludes with the narrator's fantasy of his death at the Nazi's hands. There are several reasons for this ending: symbolically, the narrator has "crossed" the nine rivers of experience and learned what each of the muses could teach him. He has also come to understand war and has found the answer to the question of why we fight. This knowledge, involving as it does an insight into man's nature at his worst, is terrible to live with. It is the knowledge of the serpent in the Garden of Eden, the knowledge toward which Eve always tempts; it corrupts, as the priest at the Sangro told him. To put it another way, the fantasy death involves no more than a kind of justice; intuitively he knew that he would journey in safety as long as he went unarmed. When he took the Luger from a pile of weapons at Buchenwald, he became vulnerable inasmuch as he committed himself to the violence of the Biblical sword, the infecting evil. Thus infected, he must die, and by that same sword. To Johnston, the purpose of life is life itself, and its end is the discovery of the knowlege of good and evil which, ever since Eden, has resulted in the death of innocence. Maturity implies death unless it can invoke a revelation that goes beyond maturity which, as Johnston suggests, can be called grace. But death is neither catastrophic nor deplorable. "So mourn, if you must," he Concludes, "but only for yourself" (492). Thus the correspondent, who is a victim of his own contraband Luger, is, in one respect, well out of it all. He will not be around to witness the cycle of violence and evil which the victors will perpetuate on postwar Germany and which will be called reparations and occupation but which will, in fact, be nothing more than revenge.

Moreover, the conclusion to the American edition seems to deny man's ability to break this cycle. The priest on the Sangro had said that men do not choose sides in the same way they choose between good and evil but are cast in roles like actors in a play. These sentiments in only slightly different form will be repeated in Johnston's last play, *The Scythe and the Sunset,* where an Irish revolutionary tells his English prisoner that it is "Heaven who provides us with our roles." The captive's reply is of special significance here: "Heaven can't ballyrag me. I pick my own parts." This is exactly what the acolyte does in the conclusion to the English edition of *Nine Rivers:* he deliberately chooses to break the cycle of revenge. Thus, it was a serious omission to end the American edition without Johnston's last word on the subject.

XVI   *The "English" Ending*

The last sentence of the American edition ("Ite, Missa Est" — "Go, the mass is over") is followed immediately in the earlier English edition (1953) by a three-part conclusion introduced by the blunt question: "Or would you prefer a different ending?"[5] The first part is a liturgy in the form of "the Canon of an unknown Mass" that is being celebrated in a cellar in the Alps. A woman with the face of the Second Eve sits in the pose of the *Pietà* looking down at the dead body of her son. An acolyte, who is also the war correspondent, hails her as Anneliese Wendler. For the death of her son, the acolyte promises revenge, but the *Pietà* warns him to "cast out / The knowledge of Good and Evil [i.e., the gun]." When he objects that is the fruit of his maturity, she instructs him to fight evil but not to admit the knowledge of it. However, in possessing the gun, which is itself the forbidden fruit, he automatically possesses the knowledge of evil. As the first part ends, the acolyte, having learned of his own sin, charges that God is guilty of the same offense. The *Pietà* predicts that some day a generation will come that will have knowledge but will not die by it. The acolyte may yet, she says, "Spit out the fruit of the tree / And be one of that generation" if he will.

The second part of the English ending is the acolyte's dialogue with the Voice of God on the heights of the Austrian Alps as the rumblings of war are heard in the valley below. It builds upon the dialogue with the *Pietà* and culminates in the spiritual struggle of the acolyte-correspondent. This is the time when he must, as the Austrian woman told him, "learn to forgive God," and in forgiving God, he will forgive himself and humanity. The acolyte, attempting to confound God with his charges, is almost immediately humbled by the Voice of God countercharging that he has presumed "to pray for forgiveness / When he has it in his heart for all / Except his Maker." By an inversion of the form of confession, the acolyte is made to name the errors of God: He has created man in frailty and endowed him with pity; He has given man a longing for life when there is only death. The acolyte's confession ends with a plea to be allowed to return to the Brenner and the death that awaits him there. But what if God has chosen a different role for him, asks the Voice. "I shall cry out against your Grace... / And say that your will is terrible," replies this critic of God. At this point when he can be pushed no further except to blaspheme, the acolyte remembers the Luger from Buchenwald which he draws and fires into the sky as a gesture of both despair and defiance, expecting only death for his daring. However, the Voice reminds him that he has no say in his own death and that he is destined to live.

The turning point comes when God reminds him that as he has shown compassion, so it will be shown him. As a choir chants the Creed, the tone of the mass changes to one of worship and praise which the Voice accepts. "Avenge all others' sins on me, as you have done this day, / And leave the human race in peace" are the last words of the Voice of God. The acolyte has come to recognize that God encompasses àll things, even evil, as he had found in Isaiah. In accepting this paradox, he can accept the inclination toward sin in himself and others and so temper his judgments with pity. The last words of God are really a command. The acolyte may censure the tendency to evil that exists in himself and others; he may even pity, but he may not judge. Now he can throw away the fruit of the tree of experience in an act of faith. As he does so, the Voice rejoices in having "harnessed the Unicorn to the plough." In terms of resolving the moral and spiritual questions that Johnston poses, these words form the denouement of the book; therefore, it is all the more deplorable that they have been omitted in the American edition.

In the third and final part of the English ending, the scene is again the Brenner; the Nazi has died of self-inflicted wounds, but not from the gun of the correspondent who has (as Johnston recounts later in *The Brazen Horn*) tossed it away high up in the Alps, a final rejection of murder as retribution. In rejecting revenge, the acolyte-correspondent is the fullest embodiment of the Johnston hero, seen first in Dobelle and later in Professor Dotheright, who will within the next few years reappear as Superintendent Brownrigg in *Strange Occurrence on Ireland's Eye* and as Palliser, the Anglo-Irish soldier in *The Scythe and the Sunset*. The

Johnston hero demonstrates in *Nine Rivers* that man can end this concatenation of evil if he chooses the right way to perform the role heaven has assigned him. This is the main reason that the American edition of the book is simply an unfinished document. What exactly was behind the slightly truncated American edition? In *The Brazen Horn,* Johnston recalls that when *Nine Rivers* was to be issued in America, the publishers took exception to the double ending as a "piece of apparent whimsy." Apparently they felt that such a conclusion might detract from the book as a serious account of the war. However, as Johnston says, they deleted "the more probable alternative ending and retained the objectionable one — leaving me dead."[6] In some quarters, the American ending was viewed as slightly arch. One reviewer went so far as to call it "a crude and contrived gag."[7] Since the American edition ends with a short chapter entitled "Uz" (implying a comparison not only with the trials of Job but also with his faith in accepting both God's blessings and punishment), Johnston is also prevented from making a point which he had touched on in his Preface more than halfway through the book and which he later elaborates at some length in *The Brazen Horn:*

. . . That all physical possibilities have a real existence in a fifth dimension which lies parallel to the four-dimensional space-time continuum presented to us today by the physicists. Thus, if he [referring to his persona, the narrator-correspondent] ought to be, or might have been, killed, he was killed. And the only real anachronism is in being aware of it in a different continuum. (336–337)

The basic idea here, that "the Past, no less that the Future, is 'open'," reflects the influence of Dunne's *An Experiment with Time* and is familiar from Johnston's use of it in *A Bride for the Unicorn.*

XVII   *Style and Form*

The style of *Nine Rivers* has prompted comment almost as varied as the form of the book itself. The reviewer for *The New York Times,* a war correspondent himself, said it was "one of the best *written* war books and also one of the strangest. No war story, fiction or non-fiction, that we know of has been written with such sophistication and (the two are not in conflict) humanity."[8] Another reviewer found the form bewildering and the book hard to read, harder still to characterize,[9] while the *Times Literary Supplement,* referring to the English edition, said the book was like a duffle bag: crammed.[10] *The Atlantic* also found it hard to classify. Actually, there are two matters involved here, the style — or styles — of writing and the form; it is the latter that dictates the former, and it is the form of the book that is so varied. A careful check reveals that at one time or another, Johnston employed — in addition to straightforward narrative — travel orders, hymns, letters, jingles, lists, headlines, cables, memoranda, poetry, dialogue, graffiti, nursery rhymes, military notices and announcements, popular songs, receipts, road signs, and newspaper reports. The style, though often straightforward and quite readable, can be wonderfully ironic, highly comic to the point of farce, dramatic and powerful in moments of deeply felt passion, and yet lyrical and poetic in very personal moments.

In addition, the book is intellectually sophisticated as the author draws on his classical education. It is a highly allusive work, not only in the various headings and titles but also in the range of titles quoted or otherwise referred to: *The Odyssey, The Rubaiyat,* the Koran, Dante's *Inferno,* Shakespeare, the Bible, the Apocrypha, Noel Coward's *Middle East Diary, The Mirror of Perfection, Parade, The Egyptian Mail,* and *The Peoria Journal-Transcript.* There is a liberal sprinkling of quotations in Italian, Slavic, Gaelic, French, German, Latin, Arabic, and a special language of international reporters called "cable-ese."

Nine Rivers from Jordan is a very special kind of war book. Compared with "official" histories and straightforward military memoirs, it may have a limited value. But it succeeds in the way Johnston meant it to, in describing the war as it was, a "confusing mixture of rascality and gallantry, of bloody murder and of common sense, of intolerable grimness and of surprising joviality." And since it does this, it succeeds also in representing more than the experiences of one man and speaks for, as he had hoped, a generation.

XVIII   *"A squib about the War";*
A Fourth for Bridge

Johnston drew on his World War II experiences as a war correspondent only once for a dramatic work. In the last chapter of section one of *Nine Rivers* (134–35), there is an account of a brief visit to Malta which was at that time a battle area. While on the island, Johnston was shown a plane of Italian design used for air-sea rescue of downed pilots. The story of how it came to Malta takes one page in the telling and is the basis of Johnston's only one-act play, *A Fourth for Bridge*.[11]

Briefly, it recounts how two R.A.F. captives and their Italian guard left the Mediterranean island of Pantellaria in search of a fourth bridge player. When the guard became indisposed because of air-sickness, the two captives attempted to commandeer the aircraft in order to force a landing on the British base at Malta. The pilot, who was reluctant to change destinations because he had a leave coming, suggested they not shoot him since no one else could fly the plane. Because fuel was running out, they landed on Malta with the understanding that the plane would not be used for operational purposes but only for "the neutral and humanitarian task" of rescuing downed aviators. Johnston's informant reported that the promise had been faithfully kept. With the addition of a few more characters and plot complications, this is the true story that Johnston fashioned into a short play.

A Fourth for Bridge was first done on British television under the title *The Unthinking Lobster* and has had few subsequent productions. All four scenes are set in an Italian military transport aircraft in transit over the Mediterranean sometime in 1942. That the plane is a microcosm of a world at war becomes obvious with a look at the cast: a German, two British, an American, an Italian, a Polish partisan, and the pilot. The flight is an allegorical journey into peace, depicting the natural innocence man exhibits when free of the restraints which national shibboleths impose on him in time of crisis. In the search for a fourth partner for bridge, the characters temporarily find the "insanity" of brotherhood.

Just as bridge is a metaphor for the peaceful game of politics among nations, war is a more deadly game in which the upperhand changes unexpectedly and illogically as it would in a game of cards. The power passes from the Italian to the two Englishmen and the American, thence to the German, and finally to the Pole. The play is constructed around these power-transfers which are manipulated first by an unloaded gun, then by one with bullets, and finally by a grenade (perhaps a metaphor for the atom bomb). It then becomes obvious that nobody can survive unless all agree to forego violence. This they do to their own great relief. Their individual confessions of annoyance with some aspect of their country

or their national image lead to the final revelation of the absurdity
of fighting when the Russian pilot explains how he has been tossed
to and fro by the fortunes of war until he no longer has a national-
ity. They have all tasted of the "insanity" of peace, but it cannot
last when they are forced to descend to the reality of Italian anti-
aircraft guns. The return to the conflict is an ironic return to
"sanity."

A play that completely inverts the cinematic view of war as
romance in the MGM-Warner Brothers tradition (*circa* 1944), *A
Fourth for Bridge* remains as valid as ever, perhaps more so since
today the "enemy" is less easily recognizable as human than "the
Hun" ever was. It is not one of Johnston's major works, but it
demonstrates that he can put more into a short play, theatrically
and thematically, than most current practitioners of the genre.

CHAPTER 8

The Playwright in the Courtroom: Blind Man's Buff and Strange Occurrence on Ireland's Eye

I *Toller for the Abbey*

JOHNSTON first became acquainted with the work of Ernst Toller when he saw a production of *Masse Mensch* (*Man and the Masses,* 1919) in London in 1926. Nearly a decade later, the German dramatist persuaded Johnston to "disembowel" another of his plays, *Die blinde Göttin* (*The Blind Goddess,* 1932) by adapting it for the Abbey Theatre. This courtroom drama, quite different from the earlier Expressionistic play, was based on a famous contemporary trial of two lovers, a doctor and his secretary-nurse, who were falsely convicted of murdering the doctor's wife.[1] Although the innocence of the pair is finally established, the doctor has become understandably embittered by this miscarriage of justice but still wishes to resume the affair. However, the nurse realizes it is impossible and rejects him, speaking out against the system that changed their lives.

In addition to being an indictment of German bureaucracy and bourgeois values, Toller's play is an attack on a legal system that condemns and punishes a man on the basis of circumstantial evidence for a crime he did not commit. Toller wanted *Die blinde Göttin* turned "into an Irish play for some obscure reason," Johnston recalled. "I hadn't read the play closely at the time but I said I would. And when I read it I realized that I didn't like it and I didn't want to do it at all...."[2] In an attempt to get out of the agree-

127

ment, Johnston wrote Toller that if he undertook the adaptation, he would turn the heroes into villains and vice versa, presuming that Toller would naturally object to such violence done to his work. But Toller agreed, and although Johnston retained only a small portion of the original play, the German dramatist not only insisted on its being acted but also on his own name appearing first in the program. Johnston's adaptation under the title of *Blind Man's Buff* premiered at the Abbey on December 28, 1936.

II   *The Scales of Justice*

Some months prior to all this, Johnston had himself been working on a radio play on a somewhat similar situation which demonstrated the fallibility of the judicial system, and he had also chosen as his subject a sensational murder trial, one which had taken place in Ireland in 1852. The central figure was an artist "of very moderate ability" named William Burke Kirwan who managed successfully for a time to maintain two separate domestic establishments in Dublin, complete with wives and children. It was by no means a well-kept secret; indeed, it was so well known that the gentleman's name appeared in the *Dublin Directory* the year of the trial under both addresses. The legal wife died under strange circumstances on Ireland's Eye, a very small, relatively deserted island just off the coast near Dublin, and Kirwan naturally fell under suspicion as a man who had taken the obvious if not exactly honorable step toward simplifying his domestic responsibilities. Compounding the situation was the fact that he was a disagreeable, unrepentant individual who managed to annoy most of his acquaintances who might otherwise have been disposed to vouch for him. After the Crown could not establish that he was a bigamist (although it tried mightily, even descending to hounding unmercifully the courageous mistress), it decided to try him on a murder charge and managed a conviction on such exceedingly slight evidence that the sentence was soon commuted. Still, he was not released and served the usual term for a life sentence, emerging finally to emigrate, understandably, to Australia.

This was plainly a case in which "an innocent man was convicted, largely on the ground that he was a morally obnoxious character, and was clearly guilty of something or other."[3] In fact, the miscarriage of justice that occurred out of hostility toward Kirwan was so blatant that Johnston felt he would have to modify considerably the facts of the story if it were ever to be accepted as true. For one thing, he moved up the time of the case to the twentieth century but without changing any names or altering the locale. Most important, he used a gimmick from modern jurisprudence to bring the plot to a more acceptable and happier conclusion than historically was the case. This radio play, however, was never given a title, nor was it ever performed, so after he made the commitment to Toller, Johnston went back to his unused script and borrowed the same legal gimmick as a climax for *Blind Man's Buff*.

III   Blind Man's Buff

In Johnston's version, Dr. Frank Chavasse, a physician living in rural Ireland, is accused of murdering his wife with a dose of poison followed by an injection. The star witness against him is Mary Quirke, a servant in his household whom he had accused of theft. Another witness is Dominick Mapother, a variation of the comic stage Irishman, who overhears the doctor, together with Dr. Anice Hollingshead, Chavasse's former mistress, trying to save the wife with an injection in the heart. When an officer arrives, Mary denounces her employer as a murderer, pointing to a bundle of Dr. Hollingshead's letters as evidence of a love affair that, in fact, ended almost two years ago. The attorneys for Dr. Chavasse explain to Dr. Hollingshead that the evidence is not sufficient for a conviction unless her love letters (which clearly establish not only their affair but also hint that he would help her procure an abortion if necessary) are submitted as evidence of his bad character. These letters will only become public if the defense attacks the character of Mary Quirke.

At the trial Mapother testifies about the conversation he overheard while waiting for medicine, and the state pathologist goes much too far in his testimony, citing not only the cause of death (chronic poisoning) but also its nature (murder). When Dr. Chavasse is called to the witness stand, he has somehow not understood that he must not impugn Mary's character. Instead, he accuses her of stealing and insists on pressing charges. Consequently, the adulterous affair with Dr. Hollingshead is revealed through the letters which then become admissible evidence, and Chavasse is convicted of murdering his wife.

Six months later, Anice Hollingshead approaches Poer, the state solicitor, insisting Chavasse is innocent. Mapother, who is conveniently in the office at the time, reveals that the medicine the doctor gave him the day of the murder was for his cow which subsequently died. Thus, he was annoyed with Chavasse and testified against him, although he did not get a chance to tell his full story at the trial. By error, he was given the poison Mrs. Chavasse took to commit suicide. Poer makes a sympathetic yet impatient plea to the pathologist to reconsider his judgments, a plea that reflects Johnston's own conviction that the law will protect as well as prosecute if the men who serve it do not become cynical. In the last scene of the play, Dr. Chavasse's conviction has been overturned because of insufficient evidence, and after a year in prison he is released. Dr. Hollingshead eagerly awaits his return home, thinking at first that they might be able to resume their interrupted romance, but Chavasse's insensitive and vindictive behavior shows he has learned nothing, and, at play's end, she leaves him.

Johnston transformed Toller's five-act play into a tighter three-act one. In the process he excised three scenes from the middle of the play, one of which showed the jury deliberating and two set in prison. Also missing is a scene necessary for Toller's secondary theme of blackmail. The most important change Johnston made involves, as he told Toller, an inversion of the characters: Toller's heroes become Johnston's villains and vice versa. While Toller's play is an attack on the fallibility of the judiciary system and a sympathetic defense of those who are its unintentional victims, *Blind Man's Buff* is a defense of the courts and an examination of the different reactions of two victims of a miscarriage of justice. In Toller's play, the main character is the physician who is unjustly convicted; in *Buff,* the center of interest is Dr. Hollingshead, the nurse-mistress, who, though not imprisoned but punished in a different way, is finally able to view the injustice with a resignation that demonstrates maturity well beyond anything Chavasse attains. Having learned nothing, he returns from prison seeking revenge on those who simply carried out their duties. He plans to prosecute Poer; he bullies and misjudges his young daughter in the same manner as he himself was misjudged, while righteously addressing the hypocritic townsmen on the virtues of justice and liberty, although really thinking only of his own small personal affairs.

So Anice rejects him, recalling that she had perhaps loved him almost enough to do what she had been accused of doing: helping him murder his wife. Now, as he gloats over the fate of his servant, Mary, who is still in prison, she sees him for what he is, a small man. She herself has experienced a change similar to that of Dobelle in *The Moon in the Yellow River;* she will not help perpetuate a cycle of injustice that would only lead to another wrong. In this she anticipates Professor Dotheright, the "golden cuckoo," who steps aside from a less serious pattern of misdoings, just as she looks ahead to Johnston's most fully developed characters of this kind, Palliser in *The Scythe and the Sunset* and the acolyte in *Nine Rivers from Jordan.*

There are a few problems with the play, however. Johnston refers to a legal gimmick he used to bring the case to a happier issue: evidence of the previous character of the accused may not be introduced until and unless the defense challenges the character of a witness for the prosecution. This, Johnston tells us, could not have governed the outcome of the Kirwan trial in the nineteenth century when "there was a much deeper regard for the niceties of criminal procedure than is the case today," simply because Kirwan would not have been allowed to speak in his own defense. This is one of the ways Johnston gives history "generous injections of synthetic credibility" to make the case believable to a contemporary audience.

Some aspects of the play are difficult to accept: that Dr. Chavasse's attorneys never made clear to him how and why it was important to keep Mary Quirke's character out of the trial, even at the expense of foregoing the luxury of denouncing her before the court; that Anice has no explanation for failing to attend the sick woman when she was called early in the morning; that she would later try to sacrifice herself for a man like Chavasse by falsely insisting that she shared the blame and that their affair lasted until the wife's death; that Dominick Mapother is prevented on the stand from giving significant evidence that at least would have provided a motive for his testimony against Dr. Chavasse; that Chavasse could be so petty and vengeful without Anice ever seeing his true colors. These few matters mar an otherwise intelligent and exciting play.

Johnston's background as a lawyer (he did not give up practice until 1936, the year of this play) is noticeable not only in his facility with legal terminology and courtroom procedures but also in his attitude toward the whole judiciary system. His views are summed up by Poer, the state solicitor, when he reminds the brash pathologist that whenever the system breaks down in an attempt to render justice in individual cases, it is not the fault of the system but of the men who administer it. Both *Blind Man's Buff* and its companion

piece, *Strange Occurrence on Ireland's Eye,* are in effect Johnston's tributes to his other profession and his faith in the way it
works. In the case of Chavasse, despite a temporary imbalance in
the scales of justice, the truth does come out, and the accused is
exonerated. Justice is achieved, although Chavasse is too small to
recognize it; nor does he realize he is partly responsible for his own
predicament. "Man errs," Johnston concludes, "but he also
repairs."

IV Strange Occurrence on Ireland's Eye

It has been suggested that *Blind Man's Buff* was omitted from
Johnston's collected plays only because of complications with the
Toller estate which insisted that he be listed as co-author despite the
fact that the play is, by any reasonable consensus, only a very loose
adaptation of *Die blinde Göttin.*[4] It is more likely that Johnston
preferred to forget his 1936 trial play and rest his case on *Strange
Occurrence on Ireland's Eye,* which had its premiere at the Abbey
on August 20, 1956, where it ran seven weeks. This play, Johnston
implies in his introduction, is chiefly indebted to the original radio
script, borrowing only the substance of the middle act (the trial
scene) from *Buff,* a play he regarded as a failure because it was an
adaptation that inverted the original author's intentions. To clinch
the argument, he repeats categorically that *Strange Occurrence* is
"a rewrite, not of *Blind Man's Buff,* but of an older radio play of
my own, which is here [i.e., in the collected plays] presented in
stage form."[5]

It is true that he has returned to the original story of the trial of
William Kirwan which he had used in the radio play, but even a
casual comparison of *Buff* and *Strange Occurrence* reveals that
when he says "the crime and the characters are entirely different,"
he may be splitting literary hairs. In his adaptation of Toller he
shifted the emphasis from the victimized physician to the sympathetic mistress; in *Strange Occurrence,* the defendant, called by his
real name, Kirwan, all but disappears. Although the former mistress, now called Dr. Teresa Kenney, figures prominently in the
action, the Poer character, now called Chief Superintendent
Brownrigg, becomes the real center of the play. He is Johnston's
persona; like Anice Hollingshead, he undertakes at his own risk
and as a matter of personal integrity to see that not only the letter
but also the spirit of justice is carried out. Four new minor charac-

ters are added who are involved in the reopening of the case, and the vengeful servant turns up in new guise as Kirwan's landlady. The time is 1937, roughly contemporary with the Toller adaptation. The legal gimmick is the same: Kirwan leaves himself open to the prosecution by attacking the character of the busybody landlady. Some of the lines are repeated from the earlier play, including key speeches which emphasize the theme.

Structurally, the plays are different in two respects: *Strange Occurrence* omits the scene of the death of the doctor's wife which Johnston took from Toller's original play. Therefore, Johnston must begin at a point after the inquest and burial of Mrs. Kirwan with a series of four scenes which build carefully to Kirwan's arrest. Act II is still the central scene of the trial, and the two scenes of Act III go no further than the reopening of the case. Kirwan himself is never seen after the trial scene, and Dr. Kenney has found him a tiresome man long before; thus there is no question of their resuming their relationship. From what one sees of Kirwan, he will not change, nor will the experience teach him anything; aside from his penchant for vituperation, he is probably the least interesting of the secondary characters.

Strange Occurrence opens in Superintendent Brownrigg's office in Dublin Castle early in October, and the whole affair is concluded during the last hours of New Year's Eve. An elderly police sergeant from Howth, the mainland town opposite Ireland's Eye, has come to the office for a routine check. The background of the case is revealed as Brownrigg progresses from a minor but curious charge of obstructing a funeral, to a drowning, and finally to a telephone complaint that a lodger has murdered his wife, while the lodger himself accuses the complainant of the theft of a ring. This is really only exposition in preparation for scene two when Mrs. Campbell, the Kirwans' landlady, visits the Superintendent's office with charges of adultery, abortion, and murder on her mind. The boatman accused of obstructing Mrs. Kirwan's funeral is also called in; Kirwan had underpaid him for the passage to Ireland's Eye on the day of the alleged drowning, in addition to which he thinks Kirwan stole his fishing knife and used it as the murder weapon. All of this is grounds for exhuming Mrs. Kirwan's body for a second inquest.

In scene three, a typical, uninteresting couple who don't want to be involved are called in; the Brews, with their son, were the other party on Ireland's Eye the afternoon of the murder. After the Superintendent has an interview with Dr. Kenney, Kirwan himself barges in, insisting that the police have broken into his home and stolen some papers. The letter motif here is taken from *Blind Man's Buff* where the correspondence proves adultery and possible abortion; Kirwan is charged with murder on the spot.

Scene four, an interesting new addition by Johnston, serves first to introduce the dead woman's mother, Mrs. Crowe, and second, to allow Brownrigg and Smyly, a senior counsel for the state, to speak for Johnston as Poer had in the earlier play. Johnston, like Shaw, is here dramatizing the points he makes in his introduction: "It is a question of the evidence," says Smyly: "This isn't a piece of literary research. It's a murder trial, where the question is not what we think, but what we can prove by evidence."[6] The evidence is thin, for a reasonable motive is lacking and can be provided only if the letters become admissible. As in *Buff,* such evidence will not be admitted unless defense attacks the character of a witness for the prosecution. The authorities are in a familiar dilemma. They firmly believe Kirwan is guilty, but the evidence to convict him is lacking. "If a man like this can get off on a mere point of evidence," says Brownrigg, "—is that justice?" Smyly replies that it is law, not justice.

There's a subtle distinction. Justice is something that is properly reserved for the Deity. We're not so presumptuous as to aspire to that. All we can do is to play a game called law, according to certain rules, and hope for the best. If it means that a good many rascals get off from time to time, that's the penalty we have to pay for making sure that the opposite doesn't happen and that a lot of people go to jail for things they haven't done. (41)

This brief summation of the philosophy behind the play, while stressing that the innocent be protected, also hints at a pitfall: even though men may play by the rules to effect what they suppose to be a rightful conviction, the law can still malfunction and ensnare the innocent.

Act II, the trial scene, is modeled very much after its counterpart in *Buff.* There is the same overconfident pathologist who is eager to state not only the cause of death but also the fact of murder. There is an unusually obtrusive jury (supposedly sitting where the audience is), humorously interrupting the proceedings in their curiosity to see the letters. And, of course, there is Kirwan, who is his own worst enemy when he attacks the character of his landlady, Mrs. Campbell, so leaving himself open to the damaging and finally damning implications of the love letters.

About three weeks after the trial, Brownrigg is challenged by Dr. Kenney who insists Kirwan is innocent and that he was convicted because he "didn't play the rules as smartly as you people did." Brownrigg reminds her that it was Kirwan's counsel who was using the law to get him acquitted when it backfired. Johnston remarked that the rule that permits the accused to take the stand in his own defense, and which is supposed to work to his advantage, "more frequently operates to facilitate convictions than to protect the prisoner."[7] Kirwan is a prime example, and it is tempting to read into this remark by the barrister-playwright the feeling that experienced judiciary might make a more accurate judgment without not only the testimony of the accused but also without the opinions of a well-intentioned but unsophisticated jury.

Brownrigg explains the case to Dr. Kenney as he sees it and why he believes Kirwan is guilty. Then the necessary series of sudden revelations is introduced, causing Brownrigg to doubt his conclusions. As one new bit of evidence is added to another, there is, very shortly, no case. Not only did Mrs. Kirwan know about her husband's involvement with Dr. Kenney, she had "insisted" on it. Moreover, Mrs. Crowe reveals that her daughter had since childhood been subject to epilepsy. The supposed murder weapon, the boatman's knife, turns up in Mr. Brew's bag of golf clubs, courtesy of his mischievous young son.

Brownrigg has in the meantime tested for himself whether or not a cry for help on the island could, as the prosecution testified, be heard from the mainland; he finds that it could not. He decides he must put his job on the line and ask for the verdict to be set aside immediately, for Kirwan's execution is not far off. For Kenmis, the state solicitor and Brownrigg's most vocal opposition, it is simply a matter that if Kirwan is not prosecuted there will be a public outcry; or, if there is another trial, it will be apparent that it is possible for an innocent man to be convicted for murder and given a death sentence for a crime he did not commit. That, of course, is exactly the point. For Brownrigg, it is a matter of protecting a system in which he believes. If there has been a mistake, he wants it to be his and Kenmis' but not the mistake of the law.

The last obstacle Brownrigg must deal with is the pathologist, who is finally induced, in the interest of truth, to admit that his examination of Mrs. Kirwan's body was no more thorough than the one Dr. Kenney made just after her death. Like other witnesses for the prosecution, the pathologist falls back on the fact that Kirwan is "a very disreputable character all around." Mrs. Campbell terms him a "low, loose-living immoralist." Nangle, the boatman, comments that he is a "dry sort of a man," and Mrs. Crowe admits she never liked her son-in-law. Kenmis speaks for most of the witnesses who dislike Kirwan when he insists he is not innocent: "If it's not one crime it's another." Dr. Kenney points out the danger in this attitude, reminding them that the law assumes innocence until guilt is proven, even when innocence seems so obviously "disreputable." "Neither of you are servants of the other," she tells Brownrigg and the pathologist, "but of something far bigger — science and justice. And how long will either of you think that science or justice are worth serving, if you ever start prostituting them to your professional reputation?" (91).

Strange Occurrence is not a great courtroom play, but it is a very good one. It is another example of Johnston's use of history to teach a lesson in tolerance where the matter of the individual's rights are concerned. It is a further tribute to those who refuse to perpetuate a cycle of wrong, who are willing to take risks, to accept personal responsibility, to challenge a good system that has temporarily broken down. Johnston honors his first profession in these two similar plays separated by twenty years, both admirable in their defense of the legal system, sympathetic in their understanding of man as the system's weak link, and finally quite positive in their portrayal of human integrity. In these respects, *Strange Occurrence* goes well beyond the conventional mystery or courtroom thriller that hardly pays lip service to the profession it caricatures. The well-made courtroom play is not often better served.

CHAPTER 9

Easter, 1916:
The Scythe and the Sunset

I *The Rising Remembered*

JOHNSTON's last play to date is the only one to have its premicre in America. During the 1950s, he was on the faculty of Mt. Holyoke College in South Hadley, Massachusetts; it was both convenient and appropriate that this most Irish play should receive its first performance (March 14, 1958) in the Poets' Theatre in Cambridge, Massachusetts. Two months later (May 19), it was produced at the Abbey Theatre. *The Scythe and the Sunset* is one of two plays Johnston has labeled "anti-melodramas." It had its immediate inspiration in his own recollections of the events of Eastcr Week which, he explains, are personal and undramatic and somewhat at odds with the conventional view of national uprisings, predicated as it often is on the attitude that "the embattled rebels are always romantic, and that the forces of oppression are totally in the wrong."[1]

Among the issues that impelled him to dramatize the Rising was that hitherto it had been celebrated only in a play that was highly vocal both in its attack on war and its plea for peace, two issues that are not so clear-cut to Johnston as they are to O'Casey in *The Plough and the Stars*. Furthermore, the pacifist sentiments of O'Casey's play are almost always given to his female characters; to Johnston, the women of Ireland have been more vocal in demonstrating their militance than the men. Finally, completely aside from anything already written on the subject, there is the simple fact that brave men at war have been an exciting theme since Homer; to the modern mind they are particularly interesting when they are complicated with doubts and uncertainties. When such

137

men are involved with the fate of a race and the making of a nation, their actions assume the magnitude of epic.

Johnston's characters are such men, and some of them realize the importance of the event that they shape, an event that has been repeated "so often in the course of the past forty years that one may legitimately doubt whether its local significance is of very much importance after all."[2] For rebellion has become a habit, and the twentieth century has seen the scythe of war mow Europe clean twice in three decades while the independence of Ireland that followed the Rising by only a few years was a harbinger of the sunset on the British Empire as, one after another, colony and dominion broke away. In this sense, the event and all it portended of that week in April, 1914, was a microcosm of a political development that has not yet reached a conclusion.

Finally, it must be noted that *The Scythe and the Sunset* is in no sense a debunking of the Rising, realistic and unflattering as it is in some of its details. The men on both sides are, on the whole, presented, despite errors in judgment, as believable and decent. Johnston goes much further than many commentators when he declares that the Uprising was to a very great extent "a humane and well-intentioned piece of gallantry" on the part of the rebels. It was the first time in three or four generations that the British Empire had been openly challenged, and although the Irish demonstrated both courage and aptitude, so did "the poor old British Tommy." In military expertise and troops, the battle in Johnston's play is an uneven one, but as a battle of ideas between the two chief participants in one corner of the rebellion, it is clearly a rather even match, the outcome of which says much about "winning" and the astonishing courage of both sides.

Johnston is obviously an admirer of *The Plough and the Stars*. To him, it is O'Casey's "finest piece of writing," and while he acknowledges that his title is a parody of that of the earlier play, the similarity ends there: "Neither in verbiage, plot nor sentiments does this play of mine presume to bear any relation to its magnificent predecessor."[3] O'Casey's work is not a play of ideas; it does not go much beyond a plea for pacifism and a suggestion that war is hell, especially for civilians. There are obvious differences too in character and setting. O'Casey's Dubliners are mostly civilians who reflect varied but, for the most part, unsympathetic attitudes toward the rebels. His characters are seen in domestic settings and situations which contrast with the *mise en scène* of *The Scythe,* although Johnston's tatty cafe is faintly reminiscent of O'Casey's second-act pub scene.

II *"Wherever green is worn"*

That seminal event in the history of modern Ireland, the Rising, had been planned for Easter Sunday, April 23, 1916, as far back as January of that year. It was "the only uprising in the annals of our island of which the secret was perfectly kept beforehand," writes Johnston, while a recent historian states contradictorily that "No rebellion was ever more openly proclaimed ahead of time than that of 1916...."[4] Paradoxically, both statements are true. "This triumph of concealment," Johnston concludes, "was due to the fact that the rebels had announced so publicly and so often what their belligerent intentions were, that nobody would believe a word they said...."[5] Everything from the Volunteers openly marching through Dublin to the specific wording of Patrick Pearse's Christmas greeting that spoke of the "coming battle" revealed to anyone interested — and evidently not many were, including most of the British — that rebellion lay in the near future. The interests of the country were engaged elsewhere; only a small minority of the population found national independence the burning issue of the day, and many were even hostile to it.

Several factors in the climate of the war years had conspired to preoccupy all but the most zealous of patriots. For one thing, Home Rule seemed finally in sight, and ironically after so much civil strife, it was the result of diplomatic efforts for which John Redmond and the Irish Parliamentary Party were chiefly responsible. On September 15, 1914, George V signed the Home Rule Bill. That its enforcement was almost immediately delayed by a second bill until the end of the Great War did not greatly disappoint its backers, for it was assumed the war would not be a long one. For another thing, the sympathies of the country were engaged elsewhere; Belgium was another small, predominantly Catholic country in the process of being taken over by a larger Protestant neighbor. Not popularly acknowledged but of some importance was the fact that Irish products were getting very high prices in English markets, thanks to the demands brought on by the war. So it is understandable that at first the Easter Week fighting did not figure very positively in the Irish imagination and was, in fact, a singularly unpopular undertaking.[6]

Patrick Pearse wanted a dramatic gesture of the quality now invested in the event. He could hardly hope for more, and it seemed he would have to settle for less in the immediate aftermath of the Rising. The odds against anything more than a moral or propaganda victory seemed slight, and it is clear now that the leaders of the Rising knew there was a good chance they might not survive it, whatever happened. Probably no more than fifteen hundred men took an active part in the rebel operations. There were, however, around sixteen thousand British troops in Ireland, three thousand of which were in Dublin on the day the rebellion began. Other troops loyal to British authority were available elsewhere in Ireland, and reinforcements could come in daily from England, so that by the time the affair ended six days later, there may have been upwards of fifty thousand well-supplied troops to use against any insurgents.[7]

Many of the Irish were neither well trained nor had any wartime experience; moreover, some of their leaders, like Pearse, had no special talent in military matters. Their errors were many, making it very easy to view the whole affair as a confused impromptu exercise of "windy militia" and "peep-o-day boys." This pattern of errors and mismanagement began well before the Rising; for example, one of the leaders, James Connolly, who was threatening imminent action with his Citizen Army, had to be kidnapped by the Irish Republican Brotherhood, the Supreme Council of which engineered the revolt. It took three days to convince him to delay his own plans and join the April uprising as one of the leaders. Eoin MacNeill, the chief of staff of the Volunteers (the organization young Maginnis belongs to in the play), who was known to oppose the use of arms as long as the British did not attempt disarmament, was not even told of the rising. When he finally learned of the plans, he insisted on calling off the revolt on Friday, April 21, but was persuaded to rescind the order.

In the meantime, arms from Germany which were meant for the rebels were intercepted and captured by the British because the date to land them on the County Kerry coast had been changed, and the ship, which had no wireless, could not be notified. Sir Roger Casement had arrived in Ireland from Germany by submarine at dawn on Good Friday to try to get the rising cancelled, not realizing a date had already been fixed, but he was promptly captured by the British. When MacNeill learned of Casement's arrest, he quite sensibly decided a second time that there was no hope for the affair and refused to commit his young and untried Volunteers to action. He sent messages out across the country countermanding the maneuvers planned for Easter Sunday. He even put notices in the Sunday papers to the effect that no parades or marches of the Volunteers would take place. He was arrested by the other leaders of the rebellion, but it was too late to rescind his order, so the revolt was postponed and moved up to the next day, Monday, which was a holiday.[8]

Once the rebellion was underway, the pattern of blunders continued. Though some of the telephone lines were cut, the central exchange was never even attacked, and communications with England were not seriously interrupted. The presses of the Dublin papers were never employed for what could have been valuable propaganda for the rebels. Dublin Castle, "the Bastille of Ireland," was the object of an abortive attack that accomplished nothing, although it might have been captured easily and held for a time which would have been a psychological triumph. Guerrilla warfare, which might have been genuinely effective and could have been sustained over a long period of time (thus pressuring the British to retain in Ireland men sorely needed on the Western Front), was suggested by, among others, Sean O'Casey, only to have the suggestion ignored.[9]

In *The Scythe,* Johnston adheres to this pattern of near-farcical errors in judgment on both sides. The picture is not of military clowns in a circus of war, however; Johnston's judgments are drawn on the basis of professionalism or the lack of it, regardless of which side is involved. The rebellion managed to keep going for six days, and courage and resolution were demonstrated on both sides, particularly on the side of the rebels who had little to fight with and much to lose. More than that, Pearse had ordered that the fight be an honorable one with no looting or other lapse in discipline, and his injunctions seem to have been obeyed for the most part.

Capitulation came the following Saturday, and the revenge of the British was swift. In his trial which soon followed, Pearse told his judges, "We seem to have lost, but we have not lost,"[10] a prophecy which Johnston assigns to his character Tetley who, as the fighting nears its end, decides that the war can be won after all through surrender to "some fool of a general." The particular fool who dealt so summarily with Pearse and the other leaders was General John Maxwell who, Johnston remarks, "had previously distinguished himself by placing the defences of the Suez Canal on the western bank, I suppose under a mistaken idea that Turkey lay in that direction. . . ."[11] Maxwell arrived in time to preside over the executions, "the least intelligent part of the proceedings," as Johnston's Tetley foresaw. "The Rising," wrote T. P. Coogan, "was less a military venture than a blood-sacrifice to the gods of Irish nationalism. . . ."[12]

III   *An Unpopular Rebellion*

In writing of the play's authenticity, Johnston noted that what he recollected most clearly about Easter Week is that aspect "most happily glossed over today — the intense hostility with which the whole affair was regarded by the Dublin public."[13] This contempt, which Johnston implies had more to do with forcing the Volunteers into decisive action than politics, is dramatized in *The Scythe* chiefly through the character of Roisin, the waitress in the Pillar Cafe. She exemplifies the general disinterest of the Dubliners in the affairs of the soldiers at home while maintaining a keen sympathy for those engaged in fighting with and for England on the continental front. Her derisive remarks at the expense of her Volunteer boyfriend, Maginnis, are a preface to her abuse of the other rebels when they break into the cafe's kitchen. One of the intruders she describes as a "yuck in fancy dress" and warns him to "leave go of me . . . or ye'll find there's more scrappin' in me than in the whole of yer windy militia."[14] In the charge of the Lancers against the rebels in the Post Office, she cheers on the attackers. When a wounded British officer is brought in, she tonguelashes the rebels: "Murderers — that's what youse are. . . ." (33). As the Proclamation of Ireland's independence is being read outside the cafe, she irreverently remarks of the speaker (Tetley) that if he "could suck as well as he can blow they'd give him a job on the waterworks" (30). The reading of the Proclamation is punctuated by the sounds of looters breaking the windows of a candy store. The looting, the derision of the crowd, and "that murderous Irish laughter" remain to haunt Tetley through the week of fighting.

The animosity of most of the civilian population was actually worse than Johnston portrayed it in *The Scythe*. The condemnation of the Rising was general throughout the country; even the Church joined in. The captured Volunteers who were marched through the streets as English prisoners were spat upon and taunted. The women in particular were very hostile in their reactions; some of them had relatives who were fighting Germans, and they were highly resentful of the "fine Sunday afternoon soldiers." But within a few weeks there was an almost complete turnabout that began with the executions of the ringleaders. Ten days after that historic weekend, on a bright spring morning, three of the signers of the Proclamation died by firing squad; the next day four more, and the third day, John MacBride, the husband of Yeats' great friend, Maud Gonne. Fifteen executions were carried out over a period of several days, and much later Sir Roger Casement was hanged in London. One of the leaders was married in his prison cell the night before his death; another, James Connolly, was so wounded he had to be propped up in a chair to be executed.[15]

This was the stuff of which myths are made. General Maxwell was accused of wading through a sea of blood. Pearse, in particular, was singled out for martyrdom, and even the ordinary Volunteers who were being shipped off to England as prisoners shared in the surge of nationalistic fervor that followed, just as Pearse had foreseen. Johnston had no personal knowledge of the leaders, but the idealistic Tetley in *The Scythe* owes something to Pearse; and Williams, with his talk of the Labor movement and his sympathy for the workers who looted the candy stores and clothing shops, suggests the Labor leader, James Connolly.

IV *The View from the Pillar Cafe*

The structure of *The Scythe* is based on four views of the rebellion at four important stages. The first scene of Act I depicts the opening minutes of the fray just before noon on Easter Monday. Act I, scene two, takes place about one and one-half hours later and dramatizes the government's reaction in the cavalry charge of the Lancers against the occupied Post Office. The extremely modest first-fruits of victory of the insurgents (two prisoners and a machine gun none of them can operate) and the reactions of the Dubliners characterized by Roisin's abuse lead into the tactical error of affording one of the prisoners the opportunity to direct operations against the rebels over a reconnected telephone.

In Act II, the amateurish soldiering which characterized much of the early fighting leads, on Tuesday, the second day of the revolt, to a consideration that they might seek terms, but the possibility is thwarted when the negotiators are fired on while under a flag of truce. Act III is the twilight of the short rebellion; it is Friday evening before the Saturday surrender. The end is in sight, and the Post Office can no longer be held. The principal matter here is the culmination of the colloquy begun in Act II between the idealistic rebel and his prisoner, the man of action, as each sacrifices himself in a meaningful martyrdom that provides the thematic substance of the play.

The single setting for all this action is a small, rather tawdry restaurant called the Pillar Cafe. It is a second-story establishment on O'Connell Street directly across from the Post Office (the "Ionic colonnade" Johnston mentions). Situated to provide a bird's-eye view of the action in the street below, it is, in fact, more like an observation post than the dressing station it becomes once the action begins. It is an ideal vantage point from which to have several diverse characters view events which cannot be presented on stage but must be reported to the audience. As the doctor describes it, the statue of the patriot Daniel O'Connell is to the left (i.e., toward the river), and Lord Nelson's Pillar, after which the cafe is half-symbolically named, is to the right. This memorial to an English hero in the heart of Dublin is an implicit symbol of British rule and thus a reminder of the whole point of the revolt.

The motif of the Pillar (which is now no more, having itself become an object of attack by an I.R.A. bomb on March 8, 1966) is repeated in the cafe interior where a single "narrow pillar" supports the ceiling. At the end of the play, as the British officer, Palliser, all alone in the burning building, joins in a piano duet of Ravel, this central pillar collapses in a shower of smoke and plaster. Both pillars are symbolic props of the English presence in Ireland, and the collapse of the ceiling signals the beginning of the end, the sunset of English authority in Ireland. The destruction of the Nelson monument fifty years later was, of course, the final symbolic touch which Johnston could not have foreseen.

V *Pro Patria Mori*

The characters inhabiting Johnston's Pillar Cafe are basically of four types with some variations.[16] The rebels are represented principally by Tetley, but Williams and O'Calligan are also rebel officers, and a nurse named Emer is a part of this group. The English are represented by the Anglo-Irish captain, Palliser, and a fellow officer named Clattering of the "silly ass" variety who invades the cafe briefly when the rebels are not looking. In the last act, the play becomes a dialogue between Tetley and Palliser, the characters who exemplify attitudes Johnston is most concerned with and the spokesmen for the two national groups. Maginnis, an ordinary soldier, and Roisin, the waitress, represent the common people of Dublin. The fourth variety could be called the chorus or commentator; Johnston has settled for two instead of one here. Dr. Myles MacCarthy is a Dublin psychiatrist with a sardonic sense of humor. Endymion, a former patient and thoroughly off the deep end, is supposedly based on the character of a famous Dublin "looney." He speaks cryptically in verse of a prophetic nature and belongs to the category of the "wise fool." MacCarthy has most of the humorous lines in a play in which there are many, but the final significance of his role seems much less than the sum of its jokes.

The action of *The Scythe* is easily summed up. Leaders of the Easter Rising take over a cafe on O'Connell Street which is to be used as a Red Cross dressing station. From this vantage point, the battle, including the assault on the Post Office, is viewed and reported, wounds are dressed, a prisoner is detained, a wounded man dies, and a plan for cessation of hostilities is initiated only to be frustrated when a captured machine gun, finally put into working order, is fired at the negotiators by a fanatically patriotic nurse. The commander of the insurgents realizes that the only way the short war can be won is by making martyrs of its leaders, not a difficult problem now that the flag of truce has been violated from a dressing station flying a Red Cross flag. As the rebel officer, Tetley, goes to surrender and to almost certain hanging, the British officer, Palliser, whose bravery the rebel has challenged, decides to remain in the burning building. Like other Johnston heroes, Palliser refuses to survive and participate in the revenge he knows his government will exact through the execution of the rebel leaders, a revenge that will merely be a prelude to a chain of violence.

VI   *The Man of Theory*

The Scythe is really a play of the conflicting attitudes of two men, with the Rising being merely the background against which their ideas are dramatized. One of the men is Sean Tetley, commandant of the rebel forces, prime mover of the rebellion, and principal of the provisional government. Tetley is Johnston's man of theory in perennial conflict with the man of action. He is a "damned amateur" as a soldier, and he knows it. Although he is the leader of the rebel forces, he obtained his military training "in the Board of Works" and has no idea how to adjust and fire the captured machine gun. Tetley is casual about important matters such as plans for reading the Proclamation. When one of his men complains that he has been told to ignore the orders of his chief of staff, Tetley's response that "We're all acting according to our lights" is indicative of the general lack of organization and discipline, as well as the conflicts in authority that characterized the revolt. His rather romantic view of military matters is seen in his incredulity that the British officer may have broken his parole: "I always imagined that whatever we might say against the British Army, it had a certain code — a canon of good form . . . that included a respect for the laws of war" (68).

Tetley's prisoner, Palliser, warns him that the "whole art of war is to know when to break the rules intelligently," and it is approximately at this point in the play that Tetley begins to learn, as in fact the rebels did, how to fight more effectively. Midway through the play he realistically reminds his subordinates that they have not "taken and held as much as a sentry box" and that their failure is simply a matter of ignorance. It becomes increasingly clear that, like his prototype, Pearse, Tetley is thinking of the dramatic gesture that would have a moral effect and perhaps place the rebels in a bargaining position. Therefore, he is not surprised when, before the middle of the week, the question arises of coming to terms with the enemy. But when the matter is put to a vote, he refuses to participate, saying he is not sure he will want to be bound by the results. His refusal implies a commitment that goes beyond responsibility to a group and stops only with responsibility to himself.

The reaction of the Dubliners at the reading of the Proclamation briefly causes Tetley to wonder if he is fighting for them or perhaps just for himself. This mood does not prevail, for the debate with Palliser about breaking the rules reminds Tetley that the fight has given him "a great feeling of release," a tonic effect Johnston found war to have on men. But the question of defeat, even with terms, brings up the matter of punishment and the possibility of martyrdom. Tetley realizes that to reject that role would be "to take the line that I had had nothing to do with this rising, and disapproved of it." His realistic enemy, Palliser, wonders why not: "It's a flop, isn't it?" (71). But Tetley's life has a meaning and purpose that he cannot repudiate, and whether or not the revolt is a failure, it has expressed that purpose. Curiously, Palliser challenges him to persevere, reminding him that a "fight that doesn't get fought out has a way of stinking afterwards" (73).

Certainly the nurse, Emer, who is in love with Tetley, wants to see the battle fought out. In the climax of Act II, Palliser rigs the machine gun for her and trains it on those discussing terms under a flag of truce, explaining that this way she can insure that the fight will continue, thus giving, as she supposes, both meaning and purpose to Tetley's life. When the gun finally stops firing, the possibility for a truce is ruined, and Tetley orders a hopeless battle to be resumed.

VII　*The Man of Action*

Since the resolution of the play occurs with the confrontation of Tetley and Palliser, it might be well to consider the "man of action" before discussing the final scene. Palliser is a young officer whose background is Irish but who has cast his lot with the British military. Considering the alternative, he accepts parole from his captors, but this does not stop him from using the telephone in the deserted cafe to call British intelligence and provide directions for winding up hostilities with a minimum of trouble and bloodshed. He is reminiscent of Shaw's Bluntschli in his assessment of military heroics as "another form of self-advertisement."

Palliser regards Williams, the other rebel leader, as a mere civilian because of his naive indignation at finding "that there are two sides to every war." When a fellow British officer, an example of the public school's legacy to the military, who is appropriately named Bunny Clattering, makes his way into the deserted cafe, Palliser begs him not to turn the affair into a military operation which will not only be destructive but will also make the rebels look important. Palliser's eminent good sense is significant here; he foresees the long-range effects of the rebellion if the insurgents are made martyrs instead of fools. He makes an agreement with his brother officer on a level both appropriate and meaningful to that rather simple soldier: if Clattering will hold off the British artillery until the next day, he, Palliser, will back his candidate for the captaincy of the regimental shooting team. In a few more hours, the growing awareness that the revolt is running down will make Tetley and Williams ready to come to terms and so prevent more destruction and bloodshed.

As the rebels make plans to surrender, Tetley offers Palliser his freedom, but the realistic Palliser thinks that the rebel leader is expecting a *quid pro quo*. Tetley is insulted at the mere suggestion that he had hoped to bargain for his life and accuses Palliser of breaking "the laws of war" in breaking his parole. In their first important clash, Palliser reminds his captor that fighting has nothing to do with breaking the laws of war. He taunts Tetley with his lack of military experience and his martyr complex, but he has begun to respect him and to realize that if the rebel leader does not continue his fight, it will remain an unexplored region of his soul. When Palliser declared that an unfinished fight had a way of stinking afterwards, he meant that for the revolt to come to a fitting and effective end, the leaders must stay with it to its bitter conclusion. If they could persist until a truce is arranged, there might be less of a bad taste afterwards to work itself out in a series of future uprisings.

But Palliser himself falls victim to Emer when she appeals to him to allow Tetley to fulfill his "purpose" in life. When he refuses, she accuses him of fearing Tetley, of fearing to see Tetley die, and finally of fearing his own death. For a few moments Palliser's good judgment fails; he decides to play her game and help "turn wind into wonderment." He adjusts the machine gun and shows her how to use it. When she fires on the flag of truce, the continuation of the rebellion is ensured as well as the death of Tetley and the fulfillment of the purpose he saw for his life.

VIII *Agon*

The Act III confrontation between Johnston's two principals consists of two encounters. Tetley demonstrates immediately that he has been learning from experience. First, he orders the evacuation of the Post Office; then he orders young Maginnis, who has experienced the joyous baptism of finding courage under fire, to abandon his role in the Volunteers and avoid internment so he can be free for guerrilla warfare. Tetley has learned from Palliser to disregard the rules in an intelligent way. He has discovered Johnston's dictum that "the man who loses is often the man who wins." The purpose of his life is to be found in surrender and the victory he sought in martyrdom. On one level, it seems Tetley has found almost everything he could wish for: his life will have meaning; his death, purpose; his rebellion, martyrs. The fires of revolution he has kindled will not be extinguished until his country is free for the first time in centuries.

On another level, Tetley is, to some degree, one of Johnston's Functionalists, maintaining that what is true is what works.[17] "How it operates" — not "What is it?" — is the principal consideration. Unquestionably, Tetley is primarily concerned that his death will "work," that it will accomplish what the fighting could not. For him, there will be no record of failure and ignominy; for the country there will be no more decades of political and economic dependence on England. There will, of course, be a few years of occupation by the hated Black and Tans and the civil troubles over partition, but in less than a decade there will be the Irish Free State. Basically, the goal of Tetley — and Pearse — was achieved, however belatedly, through the Rising, and the fifteen martyrs may very well have made the difference between success and failure. This is "how it operated." How then can one quarrel with Tetley's "functionalism"?

The answer is that Tetley, the newly converted realist, suffers mostly in a comparison with Palliser. Tetley had offered him his freedom once, and Palliser rejected it, thinking it had a price. The Irish rebel offers it to him again when he wants to rescue Palliser from the burning building. In the court-martial which will soon follow, Palliser would be subpoenaed as a star witness for the Crown against Tetley who knows he must be executed if the Rising is to succeed. "So that's the role you've picked for me," charges Palliser. Tetley repeats his belief that, though winning or losing is a matter God decides, how men behave is something that depends on themselves. This is really just a variation of the reply Palliser makes when he rebuffs Tetley by saying: "I pick my own parts" (93). Tetley's respect for him is part gratitude, for he realizes now that the firing of the machine gun which Palliser adjusted will contribute markedly to their success. He believes Palliser did not want to see his fellow Irishmen, rebels though they were, quit without putting up a good fight.

But Palliser, who always avoids melodramatic roles, had nothing like this in mind. Knowing Tetley will not understand, he admits his failure: "Who wants to be thanked for letting himself be talked into playing the other fellow's game? But we always do. We deserve whatever's coming to us" (94). Emer had stung Palliser with the charge that his courage in facing death was not up to hers and Tetley's — partly because he was not a Catholic as they were. To disprove her charge, Palliser played their game, although he knew it would ruin any chance for a truce and would further prolong the fighting. The whole action is foreign to his nature, and Palliser is ashamed of it. It determined his decision not to permit Tetley to save his life before the building collapses. Tetley understands none of this. To him, Palliser is simply proposing to commit suicide.

To test the rebel's resolve, Palliser suggests that each attempt to save the other's life, but Tetley only understands that *he* has to "go through with this," while Palliser has "got nothing to die for" by remaining in the burning building. Palliser, however, realizes that to live is to cast himself in the role of Judas to Tetley's Saviour, and this is a role, as he says, which he prefers to reject. More important, he will demonstrate to Emer and Tetley that there are other people who understand as much about death as they do. It is not just that Palliser wants to save face by demonstrating grace under pressure comparable to that of the rebels. Thinking that his seemingly pointless death will only be "a matter of showing off," Tetley reminds him that "nobody will know about it except me." Replies the wounded man, "I shall know about it myself" (97).

At this point, Palliser, who is soon to be immolated on the altars of a rebellion he cannot stop and shackled by a chain of wrongs he refuses to extend, further elevates their individual actions into a much larger historical perspective; what he sees is the sunset of the title, the twilight of winners who always win and so lose, the end of an empire that is disintegrating despite a series of victories. For Tetley, there is still the cause of Irish liberty, but Palliser is suspicious of causes, for they "always let you down." This is a soldier's farewell to arms. Despite his yielding to pride and playing the enemy's game on one occasion, Palliser is the Johnston hero, the anti-Functionalist who opts out of a series of wrongs, refusing to perpetuate the chain by offering himself as a link. If the leaders of the revolution are to be punished, as they will be, Palliser will not have to participate in it. His "no" is a high price to pay, but it is also what makes him the more meaningful character. He is also the truer martyr, for he sacrifices his life for something more than a cause: for a vision of the self, for a role he has chosen deliberately that involves no payment of debts and no remorse. Palliser's curtain line is magnificently symbolic of the promise of a renewal of life through death and is therefore particularly appropriate to the Easter season of the revolt: "Winter gives back the roses to the frost-filled earth."

IX *Saving Face*

Johnston himself has pointed out that " 'Face,' not slogans, is one of the most powerful motivating forces in the breasts of men...."[18] He insists that saving face probably had more to do than either politics or economics with driving the Volunteers into action in April, 1916. For this reason, saving face is a motif that figures prominently in this anti-melodrama. Since Maginnis is representative of the Dublin fighting men, it is most apparent in his case. When Roisin taunts him because his route-march has been called off, Maginnis threatens to leave the Volunteers. His resentment increases — even Emer taunts him with being a "Mickey Dazzler" — until Tetley coaxes him back into action, thus giving him a chance to redeem himself in battle. Emer even taunts Tetley with trying to save everybody's face but his own when he excuses Maginnis for obeying the orders of his chief of staff who had cancelled the mobilization. Tetley explains in the language of political oratory that with "the greatest war in history" being fought, when men are dying for their countries, he would feel thoroughly base if he did not fight for his own. The most dramatic instance of face-saving has already been mentioned in another context: Palliser's rigging the machine gun for Emer, an action that is really a face-saving response to her charge that he is cowardly. Even his death in the burning building has something of the face-saving gesture about it.

X *Two Choric Characters: The Doctor and His Patient*

The problem of face never comes up with Dr. MacCarthy, Johnston's funniest character and one of his liveliest creations. He is consistently irreverent on an unbelievably wide variety of topics, including himself. Probably because he is the only character who has genuine self-confidence, he finds no need to boast or pretend. He has two functions in the play. First, he is the principal means of injecting humor into the otherwise serious proceedings. His range of targets is broad: love, sex, sin, drink, medicine, marriage, classical music, England, Dublin icons, the Irish diet, patriotism, masculinity, horoscopes, clichés, and the Cuala Press. His second function is to stand between the two opposing forces, looking objectively at both sides. In this respect, he seems to be Johnston's *raisonneur*.

Dr. MacCarthy is never invited to join the rebels; perhaps because he *is* a doctor, his neutrality seems to be taken for granted by the rest of the characters. He views his country, his countrymen, and the rebellion at first with humor and cynicism and finally with a professional sympathy born of practicality as he attends the dead and wounded. In one sense, his role is the star part of the play, but, in the last analysis, he has very little to *say* that is of thematic importance, and his function as go-between is not much emphasized.

The character called simply Endymion (possibly to suggest he is moonstruck) is, in his own words, "Chorus to these large events." He speaks the oracular wisdom of the madman in irregular verse and appears once in each act. He is a former patient of Dr. MacCarthy and presumably a hopeless case. He appears first to announce the midday opening of the rebellion. The life-span of this Cinderella-nation will be unusually short, he implies ("Carriages in six days' time"); presumably the beds to be provided for "the few who will not leave" refer to the death and burial of the casualties of the revolt.

When Endymion next returns in Act II "to limn the progress of the offstage scene," he speaks of "High preparations" and predicts the destruction of the city by artillery. He knows, how is not clear, that Palliser has been communicating with the British intelligence. In the only reference to the title, Endymion also predicts the coming of generals and ministers who will bring a "bloody sunset from the east" (i.e., England). He makes one of the most significant comments on the whole bungled affair when he announces that "Victory's the crown ... for him / With the least power to engineer his own defeat" (48). These sentiments are Johnston's, and Dr. MacCarthy will echo them a little later in this act. In a campaign characterized by blunders, carelessness and mismanagement, the victory will go merely to the least inept.

Endymion's last appearance is as the partner of an invisible dancer in "a grave and dignified minuet," a dancer who is the symbol of fading English influence and authority in Ireland. In bidding goodbye to a centuries-long relationship, he looks ahead to the troubled days of the next decade. As the minuet draws to an end, Endymion implies the hour has come for Cinderella to depart. The evening romance of the rebels is about to end: "Carriages at midnight." Palliser is a "beloved son / Who sees more ways from Sackville Street than one," a reference to the young officer's hope for an early truce and a peaceful end to the rebellion. Ironically, Endymion, a real person, is the only obvious contrivance in this realistic "anti-melodrama."

XI   *The Sunset*

Johnston sees the Rising as significant, not only in itself but also in the context of Europe during the World War I years and subsequent decades when the same pattern of rebellion was repeated many times. The characters are frequently aware of a larger, more meaningful struggle against which the pattern of the Irish Rising is drawn. Roisin, probably the least sophisticated of the lot, speaks of Belgium and the battle in Flanders Field. Tetley finds inspiration for what he does in the defensive efforts of millions in Europe. If the Rising is an echo of a greater struggle, it is also a prophecy of England's fate in the postwar years. Palliser is given prophetic insight into the process of the not-so-peaceful disintegration of an empire that had taken decades of war to build and maintain. He realizes that the winner often loses in the long run as he acquiesces in the game foisted on him by his opponent. Having done this himself, Palliser can recognize that it is likely to happen on a larger scale. The death of the Empire as such is prefigured in his own death.

The Scythe and the Sunset stands now as Johnston's last play and therefore his most recent dramatic statement not only on Irish history but also on the necessity of disrupting the concatenation of revenge and violence in Ireland. Of the Johnston heroes and heroines who attempt to do this, Palliser is perhaps the most eloquent and fully realized, the most reasoned and most meaningful. If this play should prove to be the author's last work for the stage, it is a worthy capstone to his career and may rightfully stand as one of his three best dramas.

CHAPTER 10

Conclusion

B Y the time he was thirty-five, Johnston had four plays behind him, two of which — *The Moon in the Yellow River* and *The Old Lady Says "No!"* — seem destined to represent substantial and lasting contributions to Anglo-Irish drama of the first half of the twentieth century. Curtis Canfield, his first serious American critic, wrote in Johnston's thirty-fifth year that he was "the spearhead of the new Irish Drama," in whom, "more than in any other Irish playwright of the present time, the hope of the literary drama lies."[1] There have been those who feel that promise was not fulfilled. Some, like Hilton Edwards, the masterly director of his first play, thought he had simply tried to do too much to be able to realize his potential as a dramatist.

Certainly Johnston's work is uneven. After beginning his career with two striking plays which were highly praised, in the Thirties and early Forties he went on to do five more which were interesting but would hardly comprise the cornerstone of a major reputation. In the 1950s, he wrote a serious courtroom drama as well as an extremely fine Irish history play, which have temporarily concluded his career. Of his nine full-length plays, then, three are superb. In addition, there is also an excellent historical study of Swift and an unusually fascinating, multi-leveled report of the war years. These would seem to be the basis of Johnston's reputation at present, and it is a substantial foundation. There seems no reason to question the assessment that outside Synge and O'Casey (Beckett constituting a special case), Johnston is probably the only other Irish dramatist "who might stand up to serious critical examination in the context of world drama. . . ."[2] Robert Hogan goes further and insists that Johnston has more than lived up to his promise. "The promise that has not been fulfilled is that of the theatre itself."[3] To cavil about Johnston's *oeuvre* is really, in Hilton Edwards' words, to

154

pay him "the compliment of expecting more from him, knowing
. . . his potentiality."[4]

What, then, is Johnston's place in the Irish dramatic movement?
Una Ellis-Fermor believes that Irish drama shows a "continuous
development from its beginnings in 1899 to the present day, and
even the most recent drama cannot be sharply detached from that
continuum."[5] The writers of the Thirties and Forties such as Johnston and Paul Vincent Carroll are viewed as a part of that con-
tinuity. With his portrait of middle-class Irish life in a play like *The
Moon in the Yellow River,* Johnston takes over where Sean
O'Casey left off. Such a play also extends into the late 1920s
O'Casey's vision of the uneasy years immediately following the
Revolution of 1916 and the civil war. This theory is not very convincing, as far as Johnston is concerned, in that it makes too much
of one play, for in the work that followed, Johnston went in a
variety of directions, none of them, excepting *The Scythe* and possibly *The Golden Cuckoo,* particularly "Irish" in subject and
theme.

John Gassner is probably more to the point in dividing Irish
drama into a "first galaxy" through 1922 and a "second coming"
after the establishment of the Irish Free State and the Abbey
Production of O'Casey's *The Shadow of a Gunman.*[6] Harold
Ferrar elaborates on this assessment, suggesting that "the revolt of
the Irish playwright against the severe limits of his craft began not
with O'Casey but with Yeats's break from the original ideas of the
dramatic renaissance and his venture into the dance plays."[7]
Although Yeats' contribution did not leave a significant mark on
either the Abbey's policy or its repertory, his receptivity to the new
and experimental was evidenced in his role as co-founder with
Lennox Robinson of the Dublin Drama League. From the climate
of experiment established by a decade of the League's work came
the Gate Theatre productions which were to offer for many years
a distinct choice instead of a mere echo of the national theater's
repertory. It is in this context of Gassner's "second coming" that
Johnston is best seen. Owing practically nothing to the poetic folk
drama or the realistic peasant plays of the early years of the renaissance, he is really in the mainstream of experimental world drama
of the 1920s. Johnston's work will indeed stand up to critical
examination in comparison with the best of modern drama.

Notes and References

Preface

1. Una Ellis-Fermor, *The Irish Dramatic Movement,* 2nd ed. (London, 1954), p. 33.
2. Quoted in Robert Hogan, *After the Irish Renaissance* (Minneapolis, 1967), p. 12.

Chapter One

1. Thomas Hogan, "Denis Johnston," *Envoy,* III (August, 1950), 34.
2. *Lady Gregory's Journals,* Lennox Robinson, ed. (New York, 1947), pp. 112–113.
3. Ibid., pp. 115–117.
4. Gordon Henderson, "An Interview with Denis Johnston," *The Journal of Irish Literature,* II (May–September, 1973), 42.
5. Harold Ferrar, *Denis Johnston's Irish Theatre* (Dublin, 1973), p. 12.
6. Ibid.
7. Denis Johnston, "Sean O'Casey, A Biography and an Appraisal," *Modern Drama,* IV (December, 1961), 326.
8. Denis Johnston, "Opus One," *The Old Lady Says "No!" and Other Plays* (Boston, 1960), p. 16.
9. Micheal MacLiammoir, *All For Hecuba,* rev. ed. (Dublin, 1961), p. 78.
10. Gordon Henderson, "An Interview with Hilton Edwards and Micheal MacLiammoir," *The Journal of Irish Literature,* II (May–September, 1973), 83.
11. "Opus One," p. 17.
12. Henderson, "An Interview with Denis Johnston," pp. 42–43.
13. "Opus One," p. 16.
14. MacLiammoir, p. 81.
15. *The Irish Dramatic Movement,* 2nd ed. (London, 1954), p. 202.
16. *The Irish Comic Tradition* (Oxford, 1962), pp. 105, 203.
17. "The Irish Theatre — Retrospect and Premonition," *Contemporary Theatre,* "Stratford-upon-Avon Studies 4" (London, 1962), p. 172.
18. "A Note on the Nature of Expressionism and Denis Johnston's Plays," *Plays of Changing Ireland,* Curtis Canfield, ed. (New York, 1936), pp. 25–36, 479–481.

19. Letter to Gene A. Barnett, 23 July 1974.

20. Ferrar, p. 26.

21. Ibid., pp. 26–27.

22. "Opus One," p. 17.

23. "Denis Johnston," *The Bell,* XIII (October, 1946), p. 11.

24. *After the Irish Renaissance* (Minneapolis, 1967), p. 135.

25. Canfield, p. 25.

26. "Opus One," p. 18.

27. Ibid.

28. *The Land of Many Names,* tr. Paul Selver (London, 1926).

29. "Opus One," p. 18.

30. Canfield, p. 26.

31. "Foreword," Denis Johnston, *Two Plays* (London, 1932), p. 9.

32. Interview with Denis Johnston, Dalkey, August 27, 1973.

33. "Opus One," p. 17.

34. Canfield, p. 27.

35. Ferrar, p. 29.

36. Ibid.

37. "Opus One," p. 16.

38. Canfield, p. 27.

39. Robert Hogan, p. 135.

40. Ferrar, p. 19.

41. *The Old Lady Says "No!"* in *The Old Lady Says "No!" and Other Plays* (Boston, 1960), p. 35. Subsequent references will be to this edition and will be indicated by page number in parentheses in the text.

42. Canfield, p. 29.

43. Giovanni Costigan, *A History of Modern Ireland* (New York, 1969), p. 249.

44. Canfield, p. 33.

45. Interview with Denis Johnston, August 27, 1973.

46. Ferrar, p. 37.

47. Cf. *The Rubaiyat of Omar Khayyam,* stanza lxiii.

48. Ferrar, p. 37.

Chapter Two

1. "Denis Johnston," *Envoy,* III (August, 1950), 46.

2. Gordon Henderson, "An Interview with Denis Johnston," *The Journal of Irish Literature,* II (May–September, 1973), 31.

3. John Jordan, "The Irish Theatre — Retrospect and Premonition," *Contemporary Theatre,* "Stratford-upon-Avon Studies 4" (London, 1962), p. 173.

4. "Denis Johnston," *The Bell,* XIII (October, 1946), 14.

5. Quoted by Johnston in his program note for a University of Iowa production of the play, April, 1968.

6. Henderson, pp. 31–32.

7. "Period Piece," *The Old Lady Says "No!" and Other Plays* (Boston, 1960), p. 3.

8. Timothy Patrick Coogan, *Ireland Since the Rising* (New York, 1966), pp. 44, 50.

9. Ibid., p. 54.

10. Ibid., p. 55.

11. "Let There Be Light," *The Old Lady Says "No!" and Other Plays* (Boston, 1960), p. 3.

12. Curtis Canfield, ed., *Plays of Changing Ireland* (New York, 1936), p. 33.

13. "Foreword," Denis Johnston *Two Plays* (London, 1932, pp. 8–9.

14. *After the Irish Renaissance* (Minneapolis, 1967), p. 138.

15. *The Moon in the Yellow River* in *The Old Lady Says "No!" and Other Plays* (Boston, 1960), p. 28. Subsequent references will be to this edition and will be indicated by page number in parentheses in the text.

16. Interview with Denis Johnston, August 27, 1973.

17. Ibid. As Johnston put it, "The father is obsessed by the idea the devil has a raw deal."

18. "Let There Be Light," p. 8.

Chapter Three

1. Gordon Henderson, "An Interview with Denis Johnston, *The Journal of Irish Literature,* II (May–September, 1973), 32.

2. *The Irish Dramatic Movement,* 2nd ed. (London, 1954), p. 202.

3. Henderson, 32.

4. Robert Hogan, *After the Irish Renaissance* (Minneapolis, 1967), p. 139.

5. Thomas Hogan, "Denis Johnston," *Envoy,* III (August, 1950), 40.

6. J. W. Dunne, *An Experiment with Time* (London, 1958), pp. 195–196. For a critical discussion of Dunne's theories, see M F Cleugh, *Time and its Importance in Modern Thought* (London, 1937), Chapter VIII.

7. Ibid., pp. 111–112.

8. *Storm Song and a Bride for the Unicorn* (London, 1935), pp. 164–165. Subsequent references will be to this edition and will be indicated by page number in parentheses in the text.

Chapter Four

1. Denis Johnston, *The Golden Cuckoo and Other Plays* (London, 1954), p. 6.

2. Arthur Calder-Marshall, *The Innocent Eye* (New York, 1966), p. 168.

3. Ibid., p. 151.

4. Denis Johnston, *Storm Song and A Bride for the Unicorn* (London, 1935), p. 143. Subsequent references will be to this edition and will be indicated by page number in parentheses in the text.

5. Harold Ferrar, *Denis Johnston's Irish Theatre* (Dublin, 1973), p. 84.

6. *The Golden Cuckoo and Other Plays,* p. 6.

Chapter Five

1. Denis Johnston, *The Golden Cuckoo and Other Plays* (London, 1954), p. 10.

2. Quoted by Harold Ferrar, *Denis Johnston's Irish Theatre* (Dublin, 1973), p. 90.

3. Ibid., p. 91.

4. Johnston, pp. 8–9.

5. Ibid., p. 13.

6. Ferrar, p. 97.

7. Denis Johnston, *The Golden Cuckoo,* rev. ed. (Newark, Delaware, 1971), p. 18. Subsequent references will be to this edition and will be indicated by page number in parentheses in the text.

Chapter Six

1. Included in Curtis Canfield's *Plays of Changing Ireland* (New York, 1936).

2. "The Mysterious Origin of Dean Swift," *Dublin Historical Record,* III (June–August, 1941), 81–97.

3. Denis Johnston, "Period Piece," *The Old Lady Says "No!" and Other Plays* (Boston, 1960), p. 4.

4. Denis Johnston, *In Search of Swift* (Dublin, 1959), p. 6.

5. Ibid., p. 150.

6. Ibid., p. 173.

7. "Period Piece," p. 5.

8. John Jordan, "The Irish Theatre — Retrospect and Premonition," *Contemporary Theatre,* Stratford-upon-Avon Studies 4," (London, 1962), p. 174.

9. *The Dreaming Dust* in *The Old Lady Says "No!" and Other Plays* (Boston, 1960), p. 17. Subsequent references will be to this edition and will be indicated by page number in parentheses in the text.

10. *In Search of Swift,* p. 220.

Chapter Seven

1. Denis Johnston, *Nine Rivers from Jordan* (Boston, 1955), p. 12.

Subsequent references will be to this edition, unless otherwise stated, and will be indicated by page number in parentheses in the text.

2. *Nine Rivers from Jordan* (London, 1953), p. 296.

3. Vincent Sheean, "An Irshman's Brilliant War Chronicle," *The New York Herald Tribune Book Review,* XXXII (September 4, 1955), 3.

4. "The Pungency of War," *Time,* LXVI (August 22, 1955), 87.

5. (London, 1953), p. 441.

6. *The Brazen Horn* (Alderney, 1968), pp. 3–4.

7. *Time,* p. 87.

8. Herbert Mitgang, "The Long and the Short and the Tall," *The New York Times Book Review,* LX (August 21, 1955), 3.

9. *Time,* p. 87.

10. "The Fortunes of War," *TLS,* 2706 (December 11, 1953), 802.

11. *A Fourth for Bridge* in *The Old Lady Says "No!" and Other Plays* (Boston, 1960).

Chapter Eight

1. Ernest Toller, *Seven Plays,* trans. Edward Crankshaw *et al.* (London, 1935).

2. Quoted in Harold Ferrar, *Denis Johnston's Irish Theatre* (Dublin, 1973), p. 85.

3. Denis Johnston, "The Scales of Solomon," *The Old Lady Says "No!" and Other Plays* (Boston, 1960), pp. 5–7.

4. Ferrar, p. 85.

5. "The Scales of Solomon," p. 6.

6. *Strange Occurrence on Ireland's Eye* in *The Old Lady Says "No!" and Other Plays* (Boston, 1960), p. 39. Subsequent references will be to this edition and will be indicated by page number in parentheses in the text.

7. "The Scales of Solomon," p. 7.

Chapter Nine

1. Denis Johnston, "Up the Rebels," *The Old Lady Says "No!" and Other Plays* (Boston, 1960), p. 5.

2. Ibid., p. 11.

3. Ibid., p. 4.

4. Giovanni Costigan, *A History of Modern Ireland* (New York, 1969), p. 321.

5. "Up the Rebels," p. 6.

6. Costigan, p. 304.

7. Ibid., 323.

8. Timothy Patrick Coogan, *Ireland Since the Rising* (New York, 1966), pp. 15–16.

    9. Costigan, p. 324.
   10. Ibid., pp. 325–326.
   11. "Up the Rebels," p. 6.
   12. Op. cit., 16–17.
   13. "Up the Rebels," p. 9.
   14. *The Scythe and the Sunset* in *The Old Lady Says "No!" and Other Plays* (Boston, 1960), p. 28. Subsequent references will be to this edition and will be indicated by page number in parentheses in the text.
   15. Costigan, pp. 327–329.
   16. Robert Hogan, *After the Irish Renaissance* (Minneapolis, 1967), p. 145.
   17. Harold Ferrar, *Denis Johnston's Irish Theatre* (Dublin, 1973), p. 128.
   18. "Up the Rebels," p. 10.

Chapter Ten

    1. Curtis Canfield, *Plays of Changing Ireland* (New York, 1936), p. 36.
    2. John Jordan, "The Irish Theatre — Retrospect and Premonition," *Contemporary Theatre,* "Stratford-upon-Avon Studies 4" (London, 1962), p. 171.
    3. *After the Irish Renaissance* (Minneapolis, 1967), p. 146.
    4. "Denis Johnston," *The Bell,* XIII (October, 1946), 10.
    5. *The Irish Dramatic Movement,* 2nd ed. (London, 1954), p. 200.
    6. *Masters of the Drama,* 3rd rev. ed. (New York, 1954), Chapter XXVII.
    7. *Denis Johnston's Irish Theatre* (Dublin, 1973), p. 17.

Selected Bibliography

PRIMARY SOURCES

1. Books:

Two Plays. London: Jonathan Cape, 1932.
Storm Song and A Bride for the Unicorn. London: Jonathan Cape, 1935.
(The Old Lady Says "No!") Plays of Changing Ireland. Curtis Canfield, ed. New York: The Macmillan Company, 1936.
Blind Man's Buff. London: Jonathan Cape, 1938.
Ernst Toller and Denis Johnston. *Blind Man's Buff. New York: Random House, 1939.*
Nine Rivers from Jordan. London: Derek Vershoyle, 1953; Boston: Little, Brown & Company, 1955.
The Golden Cuckoo and Other Plays. London: Jonathan Cape, 1954.
Six Characters in Search of an Author (libretto). Bryn Mawr, Pennsylvania: Theodore Presser Company, 1957.
In Search of Swift. Dublin: Hodges Figgis & Company, Ltd., 1959.
The Old Lady Says "No!" and Other Plays. London: Jonathan Cape, 1960; Boston: Little, Brown and Company, 1960.
John Millington Synge. "Columbia Essays on Modern Writers." New York: Columbia University Press, 1965.
Nine Rivers from Jordan (libretto). Bryn Mawr, Pennsylvania: Theodore Presser Company, 1968.
The Brazen Horn. Alderney, 1968.
The Golden Cuckoo. Rev. ed. "The Irish Play Series: 6." Newark, Delaware: Proscenium Press, 1971.
The Brazen Horn. Dublin: The Dolmen Press, 1976.
Dramatic Works, I. Gerrards Cross: Colin Smythe, Ltd., 1977.

2. Articles:

"Sean O'Casey: An Appreciation," *The Living Age,* CCCXXIX (April 17, 1926), 161–163.
"Plays of the Quarter," *The Bell,* II (April, 1941), 89–92.
"The Mysterious Origin of Dean Swift," *Dublin Historical Record,* III (June–August, 1941), 81–97.
"Drama — The Dublin Theatre," *The Bell,* III (February, 1942), 357–360.
"Joxer in Totnes," *Irish Writing,* XIII (December, 1950), 50–53.
"Waiting with Beckett," *Irish Writing,* XXXIV (Spring, 1956), 23–28.

"Letter to a Young Dramatist," *The Listener,* LVI (August 30, 1956), 305, 308.

"What Has Happened to the Irish," *Theatre Arts,* XLIII (July, 1959), 11-12.

"That's Show Business," *Theatre Arts,* XLIV (February, 1960), 82-83.

"The College Theatre — Why?" *Theatre Arts,* XLIV (August, 1960), 12-15.

"Sean O'Casey, A Biography and an Appraisal," *Modern Drama,* IV (December, 1961), 324-328.

"The Trouble With Swift," *The Nation,* CXCVI (January 26, 1963), 73-76.

"What's Wrong with the New Theatres," *Theatre Arts,* XLVII (August-September, 1963), 16-18, 70-71.

"Sean O'Casey," *The Nation,* CXCIX (October 5, 1964), 198.

SECONDARY SOURCES

CANFIELD, CURTIS. "A Note on the Nature of Expressionism and Denis Johnston's Plays," *Plays of Changing Ireland.* New York: The Macmillan Company, 1936. The first and still one of the best discussions of Johnston's early work, with the emphasis on Expressionistic elements in characterization, structure, and setting in *The Old Lady,* and *The Moon in the Yellow River* as its thematic sequel.

DOBRÉE, BONAMY. "Sean O'Casey and the Irish Drama," *Sean O'Casey.* Ronald Ayling, ed. London: The Macmillan Company, 1969. The author's lecture at the Malvern Festival (1934); brief analyses of *The Old Lady* and *The Moon in the Yellow River* in a discussion of O'Casey's work: the two dramatists are of the "same school" and "nurtured by the same tradition."

EDWARDS, HILTON. "Denis Johnston," *The Bell,* XIII (October, 1946), 7-18. Interesting if rather general commentary on the dramatist and four plays by the famous director of *The Old Lady.*

ELLIS-FERMOR, UNA. *The Irish Dramatic Movement.* 2nd ed. London: Methuen and Company, Ltd., 1954. The soundest study of the Irish Dramatic Movement from its inception until 1911; brief discussion in a concluding chapter of Johnston (with George Shiels and Paul Vincent Carroll) as representative of Irish drama in the 1930s and 1940s; comment on his first two plays.

FERRAR, HAROLD. *Denis Johnston's Irish Theatre.* Dublin: The Dolmen Press, 1973. A recent study, both scholarly and readable, and an excellent introduction to Johnston's plays.

GASSNER, JOHN. *Masters of the Drama.* 3rd ed. New York: Dover Publications, Inc., 1954. A standard history of the drama, with one chapter devoted to the Irish; very brief and not particularly perceptive remarks on Johnston.

GREGORY, LADY AUGUSTA. *Lady Gregory's Journals, 1916–1930.* Lennox Robinson, ed. New York: The Macmillan Company, 1947. Contains Lady Gregory's record of Johnston's early encounter with the Abbey Theatre.

HENDERSON, GORDON. "An Interview with Dennis Johnston," *The Journal of Irish Literature,* II (May–September, 1973), 30–44. Highly revealing comments by the dramatist on his first three plays plus *The Dreaming Dust,* the Gate and Abbey Theatres, W. B. Yeats, and youthful recollections of the 1916 Rising.

————. "An Interview with Hilton Edwards and Micheal MacLiammoir," *The Journal of Irish Literature,* II (May–September, 1973), 79–97. A look back over forty-five years by the two founders of the Gate Theatre who were Johnston's director and leading actor for *The Old Lady;* occasional comment on the dramatist's first play.

HOBSON, BULMER, ed. *The Gate Theatre — Dublin.* Dublin: The Gate Theatre, 1934. A record of the first seasons at the Gate with brief references to Johnston's plays; many illustrations of Gate productions which are interesting and not available elsewhere.

HOGAN, ROBERT. *After the Irish Renaissance.* Minneapolis: University of Minnesota Press, 1967. An extremely interesting survey of Irish dramatists since O'Casey; "The Adult Theatre of Denis Johnston" (Chapter VII) considers him as a playwright of "intelligence"; discussion of all the full-length plays.

HOGAN, THOMAS. "Denis Johnston," *Envoy,* III (August, 1950), 33–46. A consideration of Johnston as the last writer of an Anglo-Irish drama neither English nor Irish; two pages each on *The Old Lady, The Moon,* and *Blind Man's Buff* with brief discussion of the next three plays.

JORDAN, JOHN. "The Irish Theatre — Retrospect and Premonition." *Contemporary Theatre.* "Stratford-upon-Avon Studies 4." London: Edward Arnold Ltd., 1962. A backward look over Irish drama to assess the future, rates Johnston next to Synge, O'Casey, and Beckett; very brief but effective comment on Johnston's first two plays.

MacLIAMMOIR, MICHEAL. *All for Hecuba.* Rev. ed. Dublin: Progress House, 1961. A record of life in the theater by the great Irish actor who created the role of Robert Emmet in *The Old Lady;* highly interesting account of the first production of that play and the early years of the Gate Theatre.

MERCIER, VIVIAN. *The Irish Comic Tradition.* Oxford: The Clarendon Press, 1962. Brief but incisive comments on *The Old Lady* as a satire in a discussion of satire and the Irish comic tradition.

PETTET, EDWIN B. "The Enduring Anti-Heroic," *The Massachusetts Review* (Summer, 1961), 785–788. An interesting if slightly skeptical review of the 1960 volume of collected plays.

PHILLIPSON, WULSTAN. "Denis Johnston," *The Month,* XXV (June,

1961), 365–368. A review of the 1960 collected plays; rather critical of the prefaces and *The Scythe,* but praises Johnston's dialogue and characterization in his first two plays and *Strange Occurrence.*

ROBINSON, LENNOX, ed. *The Irish Theatre.* London: The Macmillan Company, Ltd., 1939. A volume of lectures delivered during the Abbey Theatre Festival, Dublin (1938); without defining the topic precisely, Micheal MacLiammoir deals briefly with Johnston as a writer of "problem plays."

SAHAL, N. *Sixty Years of Realistic Irish Drama, 1900–1960.* Bombay: Macmillan and Company, Ltd., 1971. Johnston as a realist — a rather limited view; discusses only *The Moon* and *The Golden Cuckoo* which he finds the author's most thought-provoking play.

Index